Kaplan Publishing are constantly finding new ways to make a difference to your studies and our exciting online resources really do offer something different to students looking for exam success.

This book comes with free MyKaplan online resources so that you can study anytime, anywhere. **This free online resource is not sold separately and is included in the price of the book.**

Having purchased this book, you have access to the following online study materials:

CONTENT	AAT	
	Text	Kit
Electronic version of the book	✓	✓
Progress tests with instant answers	✓	
Mock assessments online	✓	✓
Material updates	✓	✓

How to access your online resources

Kaplan Financial students will already have a MyKaplan account and these extra resources will be available to you online. You do not need to register again, as this process was completed when you enrolled. If you are having problems accessing online materials, please ask your course administrator.

If you are not studying with Kaplan and did not purchase your book via a Kaplan website, to unlock your extra online resources please go to www.mykaplan.co.uk/addabook (even if you have set up an account and registered books previously). You will then need to enter the ISBN number (on the title page and back cover) and the unique pass key number contained in the scratch panel below to gain access. You will also be required to enter additional information during this process to set up or confirm your account details.

If you purchased through Kaplan Flexible Learning or via the Kaplan Publishing website you will automatically receive an e-mail invitation to MyKaplan. Please register your details using this email to gain access to your content. If you do not receive the e-mail or book content, please contact Kaplan Publishing.

Your Code and Information

This code can only be used once for the registration of one book online. This registration and your online content will expire when the final sittings for the examinations covered by this book have taken place. Please allow one hour from the time you submit your book details for us to process your request.

Please scratch the film to access your MyKaplan code.

Please be aware that this code is case-sensitive and you will need to include the dashes within the passcode, but not when entering the ISBN. For further technical support, please visit www.MyKaplan.co.uk

AAT

AQ2016

Advanced Bookkeeping

EXAM KIT

This Exam Kit supports study for the following AAT qualifications:
AAT Advanced Diploma in Accounting – Level 3
AAT Advanced Certificate in Bookkeeping – Level 3
AAT Advanced Diploma in Accounting at SCQF Level 6

KAPLAN
PUBLISHING

British Library Cataloguing-in-Publication Data

A catalogue record for this book is available from the British Library.

Published by:

Kaplan Publishing UK

Unit 2 The Business Centre

Molly Millar's Lane

Wokingham

Berkshire

RG41 2QZ

ISBN: 978-1-78740-284-3

CONTENTS

Features in this exam kit

In addition to providing a wide ranging bank of real exam style questions, we have also included in this kit:

- unit-specific information and advice on exam technique

- our recommended approach to make your revision for this particular unit as effective as possible.

You will find a wealth of other resources to help you with your studies on the AAT website:

www.aat.org.uk/

Quality and accuracy are of the utmost importance to us so if you spot an error in any of our products, please send an email to mykaplanreporting@kaplan.com with full details, or follow the link to the feedback form in MyKaplan.

Our Quality Co-ordinator will work with our technical team to verify the error and take action to ensure it is corrected in future editions.

UNIT-SPECIFIC INFORMATION

THE EXAM

FORMAT OF THE ASSESSMENT

The assessment will comprise five independent tasks. Students will be assessed by computer-based assessment.

In any one assessment, students may not be assessed on all content, or on the full depth or breadth of a piece of content. The content assessed may change over time to ensure validity of assessment, but all assessment criteria will be tested over time.

The learning outcomes for this unit are as follows:

	Learning outcome	Weighting
1	Apply the principles of advanced double-entry bookkeeping	24%
2	Implement procedures for the acquisition and disposal of non-current assets	20%
3	Prepare and record depreciation calculations	13%
4	Record period end adjustments	20%
5	Produce and extend the trial balance	23%
	Total	100%

Time allowed

2 hours

PASS MARK

The pass mark for all AAT CBAs is 70%.

Always keep your eye on the clock and make sure you attempt all questions!

DETAILED SYLLABUS

The detailed syllabus and study guide written by the AAT can be found at:

www.aat.org.uk/

INDEX TO QUESTIONS AND ANSWERS

EXAM TECHNIQUE

- **Do not skip any of the material** in the syllabus.

- **Read each question** *very* carefully.

- **Double-check your answer** before committing yourself to it.

- Answer **every** question – if you do not know an answer to a multiple choice question or true/false question, you don't lose anything by guessing. Think carefully before you **guess**.

- If you are answering a multiple-choice question, **eliminate first those answers that you know are wrong.** Then choose the most appropriate answer from those that are left.

- **Don't panic** if you realise you've answered a question incorrectly. Getting one question wrong will not mean the difference between passing and failing.

Computer-based exams – tips

- Do not attempt a CBA until you have **completed all study material** relating to it.

- On the AAT website there is a CBA demonstration. It is **ESSENTIAL** that you attempt this before your real CBA. You will become familiar with how to move around the CBA screens and the way that questions are formatted, increasing your confidence and speed in the actual exam.

- Be sure you understand how to use the **software** before you start the exam. If in doubt, ask the assessment centre staff to explain it to you.

- Questions are **displayed on the screen** and answers are entered using keyboard and mouse. At the end of the exam, you are given a certificate showing the result you have achieved.

- In addition to the traditional multiple-choice question type, CBAs will also contain **other types of questions**, such as number entry questions, drag and drop, true/false, pick lists or drop down menus or hybrids of these.

- In some CBAs you will have to type in complete computations or written answers.

- You need to be sure you **know how to answer questions** of this type before you sit the exam, through practice.

KAPLAN'S RECOMMENDED REVISION APPROACH

QUESTION PRACTICE IS THE KEY TO SUCCESS

Success in professional examinations relies upon you acquiring a firm grasp of the required knowledge at the tuition phase. In order to be able to do the questions, knowledge is essential.

However, the difference between success and failure often hinges on your exam technique on the day and making the most of the revision phase of your studies.

The **Kaplan Study Text** is the starting point, designed to provide the underpinning knowledge to tackle all questions. However, in the revision phase, poring over text books is not the answer.

Kaplan Pocket Notes are designed to help you quickly revise a topic area; however you then need to practise questions. There is a need to progress to exam style questions as soon as possible, and to tie your exam technique and technical knowledge together.

The importance of question practice cannot be over-emphasised.

The recommended approach below is designed by expert tutors in the field, in conjunction with their knowledge of the examiner and the specimen assessment.

You need to practise as many questions as possible in the time you have left.

OUR AIM

Our aim is to get you to the stage where you can attempt exam questions confidently, to time, in a closed book environment, with no supplementary help (i.e. to simulate the real examination experience).

Practising your exam technique is also vitally important for you to assess your progress and identify areas of weakness that may need more attention in the final run up to the examination.

In order to achieve this we recognise that initially you may feel the need to practice some questions with open book help.

Good exam technique is vital.

THE KAPLAN REVISION PLAN

Stage 1: Assess areas of strengths and weaknesses

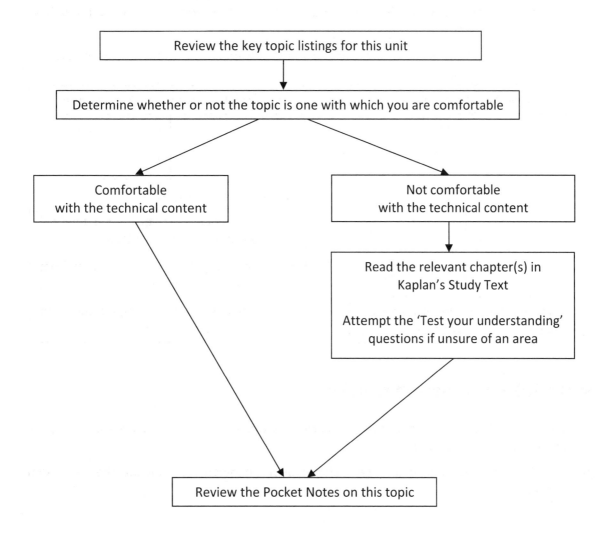

Stage 2: Practice questions

Follow the order of revision of topics as presented in this Kit and attempt the questions in the order suggested.

Try to avoid referring to Study Texts and your notes and the model answer until you have completed your attempt.

Review your attempt with the model answer and assess how much of the answer you achieved.

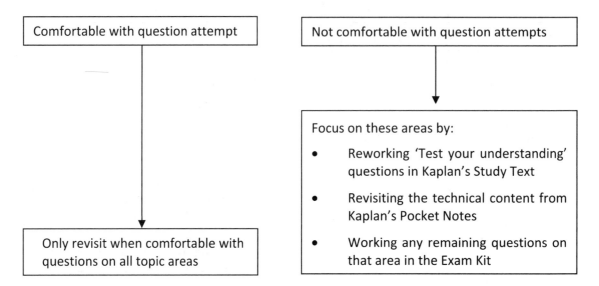

| Comfortable with question attempt | Not comfortable with question attempts |

Focus on these areas by:

- Reworking 'Test your understanding' questions in Kaplan's Study Text
- Revisiting the technical content from Kaplan's Pocket Notes
- Working any remaining questions on that area in the Exam Kit

Only revisit when comfortable with questions on all topic areas

Stage 3: Final pre-exam revision

We recommend that you **attempt at least one mock examination** containing a set of previously unseen exam-standard questions.

Attempt the mock CBA online in timed, closed book conditions to simulate the real exam experience.

Section 1

PRACTICE QUESTIONS

NON-CURRENT ASSETS REGISTER

1   SOUTHGATE TRADING

The following is a purchase invoice received by Southgate Trading, who is registered for sales tax (VAT):

To: Southgate Trading Unit 26, Three Cliffs Trading Estate Gowerton GW14 6PW	**Invoice 535** Computer Supplies plc 12 Hanger Lane Bedgrove	**Date:** 28 March X9	
			£
HP colour laser printer	Serial number 65438LKR	1	750.00
Delivery		1	25.00
Printer cartridges @ £20.00 each		2	40.00
VAT @ 20%			163.00
Total			978.00
Settlement terms: strictly 30 days net.			

The following information relates to the sale of a vehicle:

Registration number	AB 08 DRF
Date of sale	15 March X9
Selling price excluding VAT	£4,500.00

- Southgate Trading has a policy of capitalising expenditure over £500.
- Vehicles are depreciated at 25% on a reducing balance basis.
- Computer equipment is depreciated at 30% on a straight-line basis assuming no residual value.
- Non-current assets are depreciated in the year of acquisition but not in the year of disposal.

Record the following information in the non-current assets register below:

(a)   any acquisitions of non-current assets during the year ended 31 March X9

(b)   any disposals of non-current assets during the year ended 31 March X9

(c)   depreciation for the year ended 31 March X9.

Non-current assets register

Description	Acquisition date	Cost £	Depreciation charges £	Carrying amount £	Funding method	Disposal proceeds	Disposal date
Computer equipment							
Server main office	30/09/X6	2,800.00			Cash		
Year end 31/03/X7			840.00	1,960.00			
Year end 31/03/X8			840.00	1,120.00			
Year end 31/03/X9							
Motor vehicles							
AB08 DRF	01/04/X6	12,000.00			Cash		
Year end 31/03/X7			3,000.00	9,000.00			
Year end 31/03/X8			2,250.00	6,750.00			
Year end 31/03/X9							
AB 07 FRP	31/01/X8	9,600.00			Cash		
Year end 31/03/X8			2,400.00	7,200.00			
Year end 31/03/X9							

(d)   The main office has been rewired to accommodate the new computer equipment. The work carried out was completed by some employees of the business as opposed to external contractors. On the same day, the room was given a coat of paint to the new office manager's favourite colour – egg shell blue. The costs of the rewiring and the painting were:

Wages to rewire the room: £250

Materials to rewire the room: £410

Office re-paint: £100

What is the additional cost to be recorded as capital expenditure?

£_____

NB You are not required to enter any additional capital expenditure from part (d) into the non-current assets register.

2   TK FABRICATIONS

The following is a purchase invoice received by TK Fabrications, who is registered for sales tax (VAT):

Invoice 514		
To: TK Fabrications	Welding Wizards	**Date:** 28 January X9
Block 6	22 Springfield Grove	
Pipps Hill Industrial Estate	Southwold	
Southwold	ST8 4RY	
ST5 9PQ		
		£
Welding iron	Equipment no 289XP4	850.00
Delivery		15.00
Welding material pack		60.00
VAT @20%		185.00
Total		1,110.00
Settlement terms: strictly 30 days net		

The following information relates to the sale of a vehicle:

Registration number	PF07 THY
Date of sale	20 January X9
Selling price excluding VAT	£8,500.00

- TK Fabrications has a policy of capitalising expenditure over £500.
- Vehicles are depreciated at 25% on a reducing balance basis.
- Equipment is depreciated at 15% on a straight-line basis assuming no residual value.
- Non-current assets are depreciated in the year of acquisition but not in the year of disposal.

Record the following information in the non-current assets register below:

(a)   any acquisitions of non-current assets during the year ended 31 January X9

(b)   any disposals of non-current assets during the year ended 31 January X9

(c)   depreciation for the year ended 31 January X9.

Non-current assets register

Description	Acquisition date	Cost £	Depreciation charges £	Carrying amount £	Funding method	Disposal proceeds	Disposal date
Equipment							
Workshop fit out	17/07/X6	5,400.00			Cash		
Year end 31/01/X7			810.00	4,590.00			
Year end 31/01/X8			810.00	3,780.00			
Year end 31/01/X9							
Motor vehicles							
PF07 THY	04/06/X6	13,500.00			Cash		
Year end 31/01/X7			3,375.00	10,125.00			
Year end 31/01/X8			2,531.25	7,593.75			
Year end 31/01/X9							
SR08 EKE	24/01/X8	7,300.00			Part-exchange		
Year end 31/01/X8			1,825.00	5,475.00			
Year end 31/01/X9							

3   BYTES TECHNOLOGY GROUP

The following is a purchase invoice received by Bytes Technology Group, who is registered for sales tax (VAT):

Invoice 84297		
To: Bytes Technology Group 119 Abbots Close Petersfield PF10 1FR	PC Universe 13 Heron Drive Petersfield PF4 9QZ	**Date:** 28 March X9
		£
Printer	Serial number 1807G92	550.00
Delivery		10.00
Printer cartridges		40.00
VAT @20%		120.00
Total		720.00
Settlement terms: strictly 30 days net		

The following information relates to the sale of a vehicle:

Registration number	EJ09 TYZ
Date of sale	20 March X9
Selling price excluding VAT	£3,200.00

- Bytes Technology Group has a policy of capitalising expenditure over £500.
- Vehicles are depreciated at 30% on a reducing balance basis.
- Computer Equipment is depreciated at 20% on a straight-line basis assuming no residual value.
- Non-current assets are depreciated in the year of acquisition but not in the year of disposal.

Record the following information in the non-current assets register below:

(a)   any acquisitions of non-current assets during the year ended 31 March X9

(b)   any disposals of non-current assets during the year ended 31 March X9

(c)   depreciation for the year ended 31 March X9.

Non-current assets register

Description	Acquisition date	Cost £	Depreciation charges £	Carrying amount £	Funding method	Disposal proceeds	Disposal date
Computer equipment							
Mainframe Server	17/07/X6	14,000.00			Cash		
Year end 31/03/X7			2,800.00	11,200.00			
Year end 31/03/X8			2,800.00	8,400.00			
Year end 31/03/X9							
Motor vehicles							
EJ09 TYZ	14/09/X6	9,000.00			Cash		
Year end 31/03/X7			2,700.00	6,300.00			
Year end 31/03/X8			1,890.00	4,410.00			
Year end 31/03/X9							
EA55 SAR	12/02/X8	10,000.00			Part-exchange		
Year end 31/03/X8			3,000.00	7,000.00			
Year end 31/03/X9							

(d)   Which of the following could be added to the non-current assets register to improve its usability?

	Tick
The colour of the asset	
The user of the assets	
The age of the asset	
The location of the asset	

ACCOUNTING FOR NON-CURRENT ASSETS – ADDITIONS, DEPRECIATION AND DISPOSALS

4   VIVIENNE

You are working on the accounting records of Vivienne for the year ended 31st December 20X7.

- You may ignore VAT.
- An item of computer equipment was part exchanged on 1 September 20X7.
- The original item was purchased for £4,000 on 12 June 20X3.
- Depreciation is charged at 20% per year on a straight line basis.
- A full year's depreciation is charged in the year of acquisition but none in the year of disposal.
- A new computer with a list price of £5,000 was acquired through the part exchange, taking into consideration the part exchange allowance, Vivienne wrote a cheque for £4,000.

Make entries relating to the disposal by completing the disposals and bank ledger accounts. On each account show clearly the balance to be carried down or transferred to the statement of profit or loss, as appropriate.

Disposals

Picklist: Balance b/d, Balance c/d, Bank, Computer equipment – cost, Computer equipment – accumulated depreciation, Depreciation charges, Disposals, Purchases, Purchases ledger control account, Sales, Sales ledger control account, Statement of profit or loss

Bank

Balance b/d	10,761		

Picklist: Balance b/d, Balance c/d, Bank, Computer equipment – cost, Computer equipment – accumulated depreciation, Depreciation charges, Disposals, Purchases, Purchases ledger control account, Sales, Sales ledger control account, Statement of profit or loss

5   A PARTNERSHIP

- You are working on the accounts of a partnership that is registered for VAT.
- A new vehicle has been acquired. Sales tax (VAT) can be reclaimed on this vehicle.
- The cost excluding VAT was £7,500; this was paid from the bank.
- The residual value is expected to be £1,500 excluding VAT.
- The depreciation policy for vehicles is 25% per annum on a straight line basis.
- Depreciation has already been entered into the accounts for the existing vehicles.

Make entries to account for:

(a)   the purchase of the new vehicle

(b)   the depreciation on the new vehicle.

On each account, show clearly the balance carried down or transferred to the statement of profit or loss.

Vehicles at cost

Balance b/d	10,000		

Picklist: Balance b/d, Balance c/d, Bank, Depreciation charges, Disposals, Purchases, Purchases ledger control account, Sales, Sales ledger control account, Statement of profit or loss, Vehicles at cost, Vehicles accumulated depreciation

Vehicles accumulated depreciation

		Balance b/d	3,000

Picklist: Balance b/d, Balance c/d, Bank, Depreciation charges, Disposals, Purchases, Purchases ledger control account, Sales, Sales ledger control account, Statement of profit or loss, Vehicles at cost, Vehicles accumulated depreciation

Depreciation charges

Balance b/d	1,000		

Picklist: Balance b/d, Balance c/d, Bank, Depreciation charges, Disposals, Purchases, Purchases ledger control account, Sales, Sales ledger control account, Statement of profit or loss, Vehicles at cost, Vehicles accumulated depreciation

(c) The business needs to develop a policy for authorisation of new vehicles purchases. Choose the ONE most suitable policy.

New vehicle purchases should be authorised by

	Tick
A partner of the business	
The driver of the vehicle	
A bank signatory	
An accounting technician	

6 SOLE TRADER

- You are working on the accounts of a sole trader that is registered for VAT.
- A new vehicle has been acquired. Sales tax (VAT) can be reclaimed on this vehicle.
- The cost excluding VAT was £18,000; this was paid from the bank.
- The residual value is expected to be £6,500 excluding VAT.
- The depreciation policy for vehicles is 20% per annum on a straight line basis.
- Depreciation has already been entered into the accounts for the existing vehicles.

Make entries to account for:

(a) the purchase of the new vehicle

(b) the depreciation on the new vehicle.

On each account, show clearly the balance carried down or transferred to the statement of profit or loss.

Vehicles at cost

Balance b/d	26,000		

Picklist: Balance b/d, Balance c/d, Bank, Depreciation charges, Disposals, Purchases, Purchases ledger control account, Sales, Sales ledger control account, Statement of profit or loss, Vehicles at cost, Vehicles accumulated depreciation

Vehicles accumulated depreciation

		Balance b/d	6,500

Picklist: Balance b/d, Balance c/d, Bank, Depreciation charges, Disposals, Purchases, Purchases ledger control account, Sales, Sales ledger control account, Statement of profit or loss, Vehicles at cost, Vehicles accumulated depreciation

Depreciation charges

Balance b/d	3,000		

Picklist: Balance b/d, Balance c/d, Bank, Depreciation charges, Disposals, Purchases, Purchases ledger control account, Sales, Sales ledger control account, Statement of profit or loss, Vehicles at cost, Vehicles accumulated depreciation

7 KATY'S CAKES

- Katy's Cakes is a sole trader business that is registered for VAT. Her year end is 30/04/X0.

- A new industrial sized cake mixer has been acquired. Sales tax (VAT) can be reclaimed on this piece of equipment.

- The asset was purchased for cash and cost £8,500 (excluding VAT). This was paid from the bank.

- The depreciation policy for equipment is 10% per annum on a reducing balance basis.

- Depreciation on existing equipment has not been accounted for in the year ended 30/04/X0, however there is some depreciation from other categories of asset and this has already been reflected in the depreciation charge account.

Make entries to account for:

(a) the purchase of the new equipment

(b) the depreciation on the existing equipment.

(c) the depreciation on the new equipment.

On each account, show clearly the balance carried down or transferred to the statement of profit or loss.

Equipment at cost

Balance b/d	6,200		

Picklist: Balance b/d, Balance c/d, Bank, Depreciation charges – existing, Depreciation charges – new, Disposals, Purchases, Purchases ledger control account, Sales, Sales ledger control account, Statement of profit or loss

Equipment accumulated depreciation

		Balance b/d	1,900

Picklist: Balance b/d, Balance c/d, Bank, Depreciation charges – existing, Depreciation charges – new, Disposals, Purchases, Purchases ledger control account, Sales, Sales ledger control account, Statement of profit or loss

Depreciation charges

Balance b/d	3,000		

Picklist: Accumulated depreciation – existing, Accumulated depreciation – new, Balance b/d, Balance c/d, Bank, Disposals, Purchases, Purchases ledger control account, Sales, Sales ledger control account, Statement of profit or loss

(d)   Which of the following best describes capital expenditure?

	Tick
The money put in by the owners of the business	
The money spent on the purchase of non-current assets	
The total amount of capital owed to the owner of the business	

8   MILES 2 GO LIMITED

Miles 2 Go Limited is not registered for VAT and has a year end of 31 December 20X0.

The following is a purchase invoice received by Miles 2 Go Limited:

<table>
<tr><td colspan="3" align="center">Invoice # 212532</td></tr>
<tr><td>To: Miles 2 Go Limited</td><td align="center">Graham's Garages</td><td>Date: 28 November X0</td></tr>
<tr><td>428 Waveney Crescent</td><td align="center">32 Cromer Way</td><td></td></tr>
<tr><td>Wellsley</td><td align="center">Wellsley</td><td></td></tr>
<tr><td>WY4 GFV</td><td align="center">WY12 RTH</td><td></td></tr>
<tr><td></td><td></td><td align="right">£</td></tr>
<tr><td>Ford Transit Van</td><td>Registration number ES54 DCS</td><td align="right">15,000.00</td></tr>
<tr><td>Delivery</td><td></td><td align="right">250.00</td></tr>
<tr><td>Tax Disc</td><td></td><td align="right">210.00</td></tr>
<tr><td>Less part exchange</td><td>Registration number FD01 VBA</td><td align="right">(3,800.00)</td></tr>
<tr><td>Amount due</td><td></td><td align="right">11,660.00</td></tr>
<tr><td colspan="3">Settlement terms: Strictly 60 days</td></tr>
</table>

The following information relates to the vehicle that was part exchanged:

Registration number	FD01 VBA
Length of ownership	4 years 2 months
Purchase price	£12,000.00

- Vehicles are depreciated at 30% on a reducing balance basis.
- Non-current assets are depreciated in the year of acquisition but not in the year of disposal.

You now need to complete the journal to reflect the purchase of the new van and the part exchange of the old van.

Narrative	Dr	Cr
Totals		

Picklist: Balance b/d, Balance c/d, Bank, Depreciation charges, Disposals, Motor vehicles expenses, Purchases, Sales, Sundry receivables, Sundry payables, Statement of profit or loss, Vehicles accumulated depreciation, Vehicles at cost

9 FLINT FARMS

Flint Farms is not registered for VAT and it has a year end of 30 September 20X0.

The following is a purchase invoice received by Flint Farms:

Invoice # 493843		
To: Flint Farms	Tony's Tractors	**Date:** 18 August X0
Parkhouse Lane	Somerton Way	
Hinterdon	Hinterdon	
HN5 6LT	HN11 5PZ	
		£
John Deere Tractor	Registration number JT19 7PY	40,000.00
Delivery		800.00
Insurance		2,500.00
Less part exchange	Registration number NC02 3LS	(8,500.00)
Amount due		34,800.00
Settlement terms: Strictly 60 days		

The following information relates to the vehicle that was part exchanged:

Registration number	NC02 3LS
Length of ownership	2 years 11 months
Purchase price	£32,000.00

- Vehicles are depreciated at 10% on a reducing balance basis.
- Non-current assets are depreciated in the year of acquisition but not in the year of disposal.

(a) You now need to complete the journal to reflect the purchase of the new van and the part exchange of the old van.

Narrative	Dr	Cr
Totals		

(b) Decide whether the following would be deemed capital or revenue expenditure:

Rent	
Van	
Installation of air conditioning	
Repairing a window	

Picklist: Balance b/d, Balance c/d, Bank, Depreciation charges, Disposals, Insurance, Motor vehicles expenses, Purchases, Sales, Sundry receivables, Sundry payables, Statement of profit or loss, Vehicle accumulated depreciation, Vehicle at cost

10   LEO LIGHTING

- Leo Lighting is a sole trader business that is registered for VAT at the standard rate of 20%. His year end is 31/12/X4.
- During 20X4, machine 'A' was sold, for total proceeds of £10,000 (cheque received).
- Machine 'A' was acquired on 01/07/X1 at a cost of £20,000 (excluding VAT).
- The depreciation policy for machinery is 10% per annum on a reducing balance basis. Non-current assets are depreciated in full in the year of acquisition but not in the year of disposal.

(a)   What is the accumulated depreciation of machine 'A' in the year of disposal?

(b)   Complete the journal to reflect the disposal of machine 'A'. A picklist of account names has been provided below. You are able to use an account name more than once. More rows than required have been provided below.

Narrative	Dr	Cr
Totals		

Picklist: Machinery at cost account, Machinery accumulated depreciation account, Disposals account, VAT Control, Bank (accounts can be used more than once)

(c)   What was the profit or loss made on disposal?

11   FRED FARRIER

You are working on the accounting records of Fred Farrier, a sole trader who is registered for VAT at the standard rate of 20%. His accounting year end is 31 December 20X8.

A new piece of equipment has been acquired. Sales tax (VAT) can be reclaimed on this piece of equipment.

The cost excluding VAT was £9,250. This was paid from the bank.

The residual value of the piece of equipment is expected to be £1,250 and it is estimated to have a useful economic life of 5 years.

Equipment is depreciated on a straight line basis. A full year's depreciation is charged in the year of acquisition.

Depreciation on existing equipment has already been accounted for.

(a)   Calculate the depreciation charge for the year on the new piece of equipment.

        ....

Make entries to account for:

(b)   the purchase of the new piece of equipment

(c)   the depreciation charge on the new piece of equipment.

On each account, show clearly the balance carried down or transferred to the statement of profit or loss, as appropriate.

Equipment at cost

Balance b/d	38,200		

Picklist: Balance b/d, Balance c/d, Bank, Depreciation charges, Disposals, Purchases, Purchases ledger control account, Sales, Sales ledger control account, Statement of profit or loss

Equipment accumulated depreciation

		Balance b/d	12,200

Picklist: Balance b/d, Balance c/d, Bank, Depreciation charges, Disposals, Purchases, Purchases ledger control account, Sales, Sales ledger control account, Statement of profit or loss

Depreciation charges

Balance b/d	2,300		

Picklist: Accumulated depreciation (equipment), Balance b/d, Balance c/d, Bank, Disposals, Purchases, Purchases ledger control account, Sales, Sales ledger control account, Statement of profit or loss

(d)   A piece of machinery was bought for £9,000, had accumulated depreciation of £4,500 and was disposed of in a part exchange arrangement. A profit of £1,000 was made on the disposal of the machinery. What was the part exchange allowance received? Ignore VAT.

....

(e)   Computer equipment was bought for £1,000. Depreciation is charged at 20% diminishing (reducing) balance. What is the carrying amount of the computer equipment after 3 years?

....

12 UNITS OF PRODUCTION METHOD

- You are working on the accounts of a sole trader that is not registered for VAT.
- A new machine has been acquired.
- The cost was £120,000 this was paid from the bank.
- The residual value is expected to be £10,000.
- The depreciation policy for machinery is the units of production method.
- The expected production of this new piece of machinery was 1,000,000 units.
- For the year ended 31 December 20X9 the machine was used to produce 50,000 units.

Make entries to account for:

(a)   The purchase of the new machinery.

(b)   The depreciation on the new machinery.

On each account, show clearly the balance carried down or transferred to the statement of profit or loss.

Machinery at cost

Picklist: Balance b/d, Balance c/d, Bank, Depreciation charges, Disposals, Machinery at cost, Machinery accumulated depreciation, Purchases, Purchases ledger control account, Sales, Sales ledger control account, Statement of profit or loss

Machinery accumulated depreciation

Picklist: Balance b/d, Balance c/d, Bank, Depreciation charges, Disposals, Machinery at cost, Machinery accumulated depreciation, Purchases, Purchases ledger control account, Sales, Sales ledger control account, Statement of profit or loss

Depreciation charges

Picklist: Balance b/d, Balance c/d, Bank, Depreciation charges, Disposals, Machinery at cost, Machinery accumulated depreciation, Purchases, Purchases ledger control account, Sales, Sales ledger control account, Statement of profit or loss

ACCOUNTING FOR ACCRUALS AND PREPAYMENTS OF INCOME AND EXPENSES

13 EXPENSES LEDGER ACCOUNTS (1)

You are given the following information (ignore VAT):

Balances as at:	1 April 20X0 £
Accrual for administration expenses	790
Prepayment for selling expenses	475

The bank summary for the year shows payments for administration expenses of £7,190. Included in this figure is £2,700 for the quarter ended 31 May 20X1.

(a) Prepare the administration expenses account for the year ended 31 March 20X1 and close it off by showing the transfer to the statement of profit or loss.

Administration expenses

The bank summary for the year shows payments for selling expenses of £7,900. In April 20X1, £900 was paid for selling expenses incurred in March 20X1.

(b) Prepare the selling expenses account for the year ended 31 March 20X1 and close it off by showing the transfer to the statement of profit or loss.

Selling expenses

You have the following extract of balances from the general ledger.

(c) Using your answers to (a) and (b), and the figures given below, enter amounts in the appropriate column for the accounts shown.

Extract from trial balance as at 31 March 20X1.

Account	£	Dr £	Cr £
Accruals			
Capital	6,000		
Wages and salaries	850		
Selling expenses			
Drawings	11,000		
Administration expenses			
Interest received	70		
Machinery at cost	5,600		
Machinery accumulated depreciation	4,200		
Prepayments			

14 EXPENSES LEDGER ACCOUNTS (2)

You are given the following information (ignore VAT):

Balances as at:	1 April 20X5 £
Accrual for electricity expenses	2,815
Prepayment for rental expenses	6,250

The bank summary for the year shows payments for electricity expenses of £10,539. Included in this figure is £2,358 for the quarter ended 31 May 20X6.

(a) Prepare the electricity expenses account for the year ended 31 March 20X6 and close it off by showing the transfer to the statement of profit or loss.

Electricity expenses

The bank summary for the year shows payments for rental expenses of £62,500. In April 20X6, £6,250 was paid late relating to March 20X6 rent.

(b) Prepare the rental expenses account for the year ended 31 March 20X6 and close it off by showing the transfer to the statement of profit or loss.

Rental expenses

You have the following extract of balances from the general ledger.

(c) Using your answers to (a) and (b), and the figures given below, enter amounts in the appropriate column for the accounts shown.

Extract from trial balance as at 31 March 20X6.

Account	£	Dr £	Cr £
Accruals			
Accumulated depreciation – Office equipment	17,921		
Depreciation charge	3,805		
Drawings	22,400		
Electricity			
Interest received	129		
Office equipment – cost	42,784		
Rental			
Stationery	2,800		
Prepayments			

15 EXPENSES LEDGER ACCOUNTS (3)

You have the following information (ignore VAT):

Balances as at:	1 Jan 20X8 £
Accrual for telephone expenses	4,375
Prepayment for rates expenses	5,000

The bank summary for the year shows payments for telephone expenses of £12,645. Included in this figure is £4,278 for the quarter ended 31 Jan 20X9.

(a)   Prepare the telephone expenses account for the year ended 31 December 20X8 and close it off by showing the transfer to the statement of profit or loss.

Telephone expenses

The bank summary for the year shows payments for rates expenses of £82,750. In January 20X9, £8,250 was paid late relating to December 20X8 rates.

(b)   Prepare the rates expenses account for the year ended 31 December 20X8 and close it off by showing the transfer to the statement of profit or loss.

Rates expenses

You have the following extract of balances from the general ledger.

(c)   Using your answers to (a) and (b), and the figures given below, enter amounts in the appropriate column for the accounts shown.

Extract from trial balance as at 31 December 20X8

Account	£	Dr £	Cr £
Accruals			
Accumulated depreciation – Machinery	15,437		
Bank charges	2,897		
Capital	27,000		
Discounts allowed	520		
Light and heat	4,000		
Machinery – cost	41,697		
Prepayments			
Rates			
Telephone			

16 INCOME AND EXPENSES LEDGER ACCOUNTS (1)

You are working on the accounting records of a business for the year ended 31 March 20X8. In this task you may ignore VAT.

You have the following information:

The balance on the commission receivable account at the beginning of the financial year is £3,200. This represents an accrual for commission receivable at the end of the year on 31 March 20X7. The bank summary for the year shows receipts for commission receivable of £22,800. The commission receivable account has been correctly adjusted for £2,800 commission for the quarter ended 31 March 20X8. This was received into the bank and entered into our accounting records on 21 April 20X8. Double entry is done in the general ledger.

(a) Complete the following statements:

On 01/04/X7, the commission receivable account shows a _____ (debit/credit) balance of £_____. On 31/03/X8 the commission receivable account shows an adjustment for_____ (accrued income/prepaid income/accrued expenses/prepaid expenses) of £_____.

(b) Calculate the commission receivable for the year ended 31 March 20X8:

£_____.

(c) The bank summary for the year shows payments for telephone expenses of £1,896.

Update the telephone expense account for this, showing clearly the amount transferred to the statement of profit or loss.

Telephone expenses

Reversal of prepaid expenses	125		

(d) You now find a bill related to telephone expenses that has not been included in the accounting records. The bill totals £330 and relates to the three month period ending 31 May 20X8. Taking into account this information, complete the following statements, please note you are not required to go back and amend your answer to part (c).

The amount to be transferred to the statement of profit or loss for telephone expenses will be £_____ _____ (greater/less) than the figure in (c).

Telephone expenses will show as a _____ (debit/credit) balance in the statement of profit or loss account in the general ledger.

17 INCOME AND EXPENSES LEDGER ACCOUNTS (2)

You are working on the accounting records of a business for the year ended 31 December 20X8. In this task you may ignore VAT.

You have the following information:

The balance on the rental income account at the beginning of the financial year is £1,800. This represents prepaid rental income at the end of the year on 31 December 20X7. The bank summary for the year shows receipts for rent of £18,000. As part of the £18,000 received during the year, £2,000 was received that relates to a rental income for the next financial year. The rental income has been correctly adjusted for this amount. Double entry is done in the general ledger.

(a)   Complete the following statements:

On 01/01/X8, the rental income account shows a _____ (debit/credit) balance of £_____. On 31/12/X8 the rental income account shows an adjustment for_____ (accrued income/prepaid income/accrued expenses/prepaid expenses) of £_____.

(b)   Calculate the rental income for the year ended 31 December 20X8: £_____

(c)   The bank summary for the year shows payments for office expenses of £2,600.

Update the office expenses account for this, showing clearly the amount transferred to the statement of profit or loss.

Office expenses

		Reversal of accrued expenses	120

(d)   You now find a bill related for secretarial services that has not been included in the accounting records. The bill totals £1,200 and relates to the three month period ending 31 January 20X9. Taking into account this information, complete the following statements (please note you are not required to go back and amend your answer to part (c).

The amount to be transferred to the statement of profit or loss for office expenses will be £_____ _____ (greater/less) than the figure in (c).

Office expenses will show as a _____ (debit/credit) balance in the statement of profit or loss in the general ledger.

18   COLETTE

You are working on the accounting records of Colette, a sole trader with a financial year end of 31 December 20X8. Ignore VAT.

You are provided with the following information relating to general expenses.

- The balance on the general expenses account as at the beginning of the financial year was £1,000, this represents an amount incurred in the prior year.

- The cashbook for the year shows general expenses of £8,500 have been paid during 20X8.

- General expenses have been adjusted for an expense of £750 which was paid for in December 20X8 but which relates to January 20X9.

(a)   Show how the general expenses account in the general ledger looked at the beginning of the financial year. You should insert ONE date, ONE description and ONE amount in the correct position in the ledger account.

General expenses

Date	Description	Dr	Date	Description	Cr

Date picklist: 31/12/20X7, 1/1/20X8, 31/12/20X8

Description picklist: Prepaid expenses reversal, Accrued expenses reversal

Amount picklist: £750, £1,000

(b)   Complete the following statement.

On the 31st December 20X8 the general ledger account for general expenses shows a [   ] (debit/credit) entry for [   ] (accrued expenses/prepaid expenses) carried down of £[   ] .

(c)   Calculate the general expenses balance for the year ended 31 December 20X8.

£[   ] .

19   MAIKI

You are working on the accounting records of Maiki, a sole trader with a financial year end of 31 March 20X7. Ignore VAT.

You are provided with the following information relating to sundry expenses.

- The balance on the sundry expenses account at the beginning of the financial year was £1,500 which represents an amount paid in advance.

- The cashbook for the year shows sundry expenses of £11,500 have been paid.

- Sundry expenses have been adjusted for an expense of £500 which was paid for in April 20X7 but which relates to March 20X7.

(a)   Show how the sundry expenses account in the general ledger looked at the beginning of the financial year. You should insert ONE date, ONE description and ONE amount in the correct position in the ledger account.

Sundry expenses

Date	Description	Dr	Date	Description	Cr

Date picklist: 31/3/20X6, 1/4/20X6, 31/3/20X7

Description picklist: Prepaid expenses reversal, Accrued expenses reversal

Amount picklist: £500, £1,500

(b) Complete the following statement.

On the 31st March 20X7 the general ledger account for sundry expenses shows a ⬚ (debit/credit) entry for ⬚ (accrued expenses/prepaid expenses) carried down of £⬚.

(c) Calculate the sundry expenses balance for the year ended 31 March 20X7.

£⬚.

20 RENT EXPENSE

You are given the following information (ignore VAT):

(a) Rent paid on 1 January 20X6 for the year to 31 December 20X6 was £1,800 and rent paid on 1 January 20X7 for the year to 31 December 20X7 was £2,400. The rent expense as shown in the statement of profit or loss for the year ended 30 September 20X7 and the prepayment at that date, would be:

Statement of profit or loss: £..................

Prepayment: £..................

(b) The electricity account for the year ended 30 September 20X7 was as follows:

Opening balance for electricity accrued at 1 October 20X6	£200
Payments made during the year:	
1 December for 3 months to 30 November 20X6	£600
1 March 20X7 for 3 months to 28 February 20X7	£800
1 June 20X7 for 3 months to 31 May 20X7	£750
1 September 20X7 for 3 months to 31 August 20X7	£525

What is the appropriate entry for electricity?

Accrued at 30 September 20X7	Charge to the statement of profit or loss year ended 30 September 20X7
£	£

(c)   Using your answers to (a) and (b), and the figures given below, enter amounts in the appropriate column for the accounts shown.

Extract from trial balance as at 30 September 20X7.

Account	£	Dr £	Cr £
Accruals			
Capital	100,000		
Wages and salaries	25,000		
Rental expense			
Drawings	5,000		
Electricity expense			
Interest paid	950		
Computer equipment at cost	4,575		
Computer equipment accumulated depreciation	1,550		
Prepayments			

21   RENTAL EXPENSES

The policy of the business for accruals and prepayments is as follows:

An entry is made into the income or expense account and an opposite entry into the relevant asset or liability account. In the following period the entry is reversed.

You are looking at rental expenses for the year ended 31 March 20X7.

The cash book for the year shows payments for rent of £10,550.

This includes payments for 2 properties as follows:

Rental for the period:

Property A: 1 January to 31 December 20X7 £1,500

Property B: 1 April 20X7 to 31 March 20X8 £2,900

(a)   Calculate the value of the adjustment required for rental expenses as at 31 March 20X7.

(b)   Update the rental expenses account. You must show:

- the cash book figure
- the year-end adjustment
- the transfer to the statement or profit or loss for the year.

Rental expenses

Prepaid expenses (reversal)	1,800		

Picklist: Accrued expenses, Bank, Prepaid expenses, Rent, Statement of profit or loss

RECONCILIATIONS

22 BANK RECONCILIATION (1)

The bank statement has been compared with the cash book and the following differences identified:

1 Bank interest paid of £82 was not entered in the cash book.

2 A cheque paid for £450 has been incorrectly entered in the cash book as £540.

3 Cheques totalling £1,980 paid into the bank at the end of the month are not showing on the bank statement.

4 A BACS receipt of £1,750 from a customer has not been entered in the cash book.

The balance showing on the bank statement is a credit of £5,250 and the balance in the cash book is a debit of £5,472.

Use the following table to show the THREE adjustments you need to make to the cash book.

Adjustment	Amount £	Debit/Credit

23   BANK RECONCILIATION (2)

The bank statement has been compared with the cash book and the following differences identified:

1   Cheques totalling £1,629 paid into the bank at the end of the month are not showing on the bank statement.

2   Bank interest paid of £106 was not entered in the cash book.

3   A cheque for £350 written on 2 June has been incorrectly entered in the cash book at 2 May.

4   A receipt from a customer of £1,645 has cleared the bank but has not been entered in the cash book.

The balance showing on the bank statement at 31 May is a credit of £363 and the balance in the cash book is a debit of £103.

Use the following table to show the THREE adjustments you need to make to the cash book.

Adjustment	Amount £	Debit/Credit

24   BANK RECONCILIATION (3)

Which three of the following differences between a company's cashbook balance and its bank statement balance as at 30 November 20X9 would feature in the bank reconciliation statement:

(i)   Cheques recorded and sent to suppliers before 30 November 20X9 but not yet presented for payment.

(ii)   Omission by the bank of a lodgement made by the company on 26 November 20X9.

(iii)   Bank charges.

(iv)   Cheques paid in before 30 November 20X9 but not credited by the bank until 3 December 20X9.

(v)   A customer's cheque recorded and paid in before 30 November 20X9 but dishonoured by the bank.

–   i, ii, iii

–   i, iii, v

–   i, ii, iv

–   iii, iv, v

25 PURCHASES LEDGER CONTROL ACCOUNT

You are working on the final accounts of a business.

You have the following information:

(a) A payment of £4,185 to a supplier has been credited to the supplier's account in the purchases ledger.

(b) A supplier with a balance of £2,170 has been listed as £2,710.

(c) A credit purchase of £750 (including VAT) has not been included in the relevant supplier's account in the purchase ledger.

(d) A casting error has been made and one of the supplier accounts has been undercast by £462.

(e) A supplier account with a balance of £1,902 has been omitted from the list.

(f) Purchase returns totalling £540 has been entered twice in error.

You now need to make the appropriate adjustments in the table below. For each adjustment clearly state the amount and whether the item should be added or subtracted from the list of balances.

	Add/Subtract	£
Total from list of balances		52,750
Adjustment for (a)		
Adjustment for (b)		
Adjustment for (c)		
Adjustment for (d)		
Adjustment for (e)		
Adjustment for (f)		
Revised total to agree with PLCA		47,494

26 PURCHASES LEDGER CONTROL ACCOUNT (2)

You are working on the final accounts of a business

You have the following information:

(a) A payment of £1,277 to a supplier has been debited to the supplier's account in the purchases ledger as £1,722.

(b) A supplier with a debit balance of £2,170 has been listed as a credit balance.

(c) A credit purchase return of £1,000 (net of VAT at 20%) has not been included in the relevant supplier's account in the purchase ledger.

(d) A casting error has been made and one of the supplier accounts has been overcast by £132.

(e) A supplier account with a balance of £2,100 has been omitted from the list.

(f) A credit purchase has been entered into the individual account net of VAT at 20%. The net amount is £600.

You now need to make the appropriate adjustments in the table below. For each adjustment clearly state the amount and whether the item should be added or subtracted from the list of balances.

	Add/Subtract	£
Total from list of balances		132,589
Adjustment for (a)		
Adjustment for (b)		
Adjustment for (c)		
Adjustment for (d)		
Adjustment for (e)		
Adjustment for (f)		
Revised total to agree with PLCA		129,582

27 SALES LEDGER CONTROL ACCOUNT

You are working on the final accounts of a business.

You have the following information:

(a) A casting error has been made and one of the customer accounts has been overcast by £73.

(b) Sales returns totalling £280 has been entered twice in error.

(c) A receipt of £2,771 from a customer has been debited to the customer's account in the sales ledger.

(d) A credit sale of £3,090 (including VAT) has not been included in the relevant customer's account in the sales ledger.

(e) A customer account with a balance of £935 has been omitted from the list.

(f) A customer with a balance of £4,725 has been listed as £4,275.

You now need to make the appropriate adjustments in the table below. For each adjustment clearly state the amount and whether the item should be added or subtracted from the list of balances.

	Add/Subtract	£
Total from list of balances		31,820
Adjustment for (a)		
Adjustment for (b)		
Adjustment for (c)		
Adjustment for (d)		
Adjustment for (e)		
Adjustment for (f)		
Revised total to agree with SLCA		30,960

28 SALES LEDGER CONTROL ACCOUNT (2)

You are working on the final accounts of a business.

You have the following information:

(a) A casting error has been made and one of the customer accounts has been undercast by £65.

(b) Sales returns totalling £280 have not been entered in a customer's individual ledger.

(c) A receipt of £1,300 from a customer has been credited to the customer's account in the sales ledger as 130.

(d) A credit sale of £3,000 (excluding VAT at 20%) has not been included in the relevant customer's account in the sales ledger.

(e) A customer account with a balance of £99 has been duplicated in the list of balances.

(f) A customer with a credit balance of £50 has been listed as a debit balance of £50.

You now need to make the appropriate adjustments in the table below. For each adjustment clearly state the amount and whether the item should be added or subtracted from the list of balances. If no adjustment is required enter '0' into the amount column.

	Add/Subtract	£
Total from list of balances		31,100
Adjustment for (a)		
Adjustment for (b)		
Adjustment for (c)		
Adjustment for (d)		
Adjustment for (e)		
Adjustment for (f)		
Revised total to agree with SLCA		33,116

29 ANDREAS

You are working on the accounting records of Andreas with a year end of 30 June 20X6. You have five extracts from the ledger accounts for the year ended 30 June 20X6. You need to start preparing the trial balance as at 30 June 20X6.

Discounts received

Date	Description	Dr (£)	Date	Description	Cr (£)
			30/6/X6	Bal b/f	300

Irrecoverable debts expense

Date	Description	Dr (£)	Date	Description	Cr (£)
30/6/X6	Bal b/f	1,987			

Rental income

Date	Description	Dr (£)	Date	Description	Cr (£)
			30/6/X6	Bal b/f	3,000

The rental income balance has already been adjusted for prepaid income of £500

Electricity

Date	Description	Dr (£)	Date	Description	Cr (£)
30/6/X6	Bal b/f	450			

Electricity expense needs to be adjusted for a prepaid expense of £100

Bank

Date	Description	Dr (£)	Date	Description	Cr (£)
30/6/X6	Bal b/f	11,000			

There were no other accruals or prepayments of income or expense other than those detailed above.

(a)   Using all the information given above and the balances given in the table below, enter the amounts into the appropriate trial balance columns for the accounts shown.

Extract from trial balance as at 30 June 20X6.

Account	£	Dr £	Cr £
Bank			
Capital	24,198		
Discounts received			
Electricity			
Fixtures & fittings at cost	11,000		
Fixtures & fittings accumulated depreciation	2,400		
Irrecoverable debt expense			
Misc. expense	2,600		
Prepaid expense			
Prepaid income			
Rental income			
Stationery	55		

You are now ready to prepare the reconciliation of the sales ledger control account (receivables control account) to the sales ledger.

The total of the balance on the sales ledger control account is £9,500 compared to the total of the balances on the sales ledger being £9,507. On investigation the following errors have been discovered:

1 A customer account with a debit balance of £157 was duplicated in error.

2 A contra entry for £100 was not made in the subsidiary (memorandum) ledger or the control account in the general ledger.

3 A sales return of £350 from a customer was not posted in the sales ledger control account in the general ledger.

4 The discounts allowed total of £200 was entered twice into the sales ledger control account.

(b) Use the following table to show the TWO adjustments required to the listing of the SALES ledger. For the 'Add' and 'Deduct' columns, tick as appropriate.

Adjustment number	Amount (£)	Add	Deduct

(c) Use the following table to show the THREE adjustments required to the SALES LEDGER CONTROL account in the GENERAL ledger. For the 'Debit' and 'Credit' columns, tick as appropriate.

Adjustment number	Amount (£)	Debit	Credit

30 KYLE

You are working on the accounting records of Kyle with a year end of 31 December. You have five extracts from the ledger accounts for the year ended 31 December 20X6. You need to start preparing the trial balance as at 31 December 20X6.

Allowance for doubtful debts adjustment

Date	Description	Dr (£)	Date	Description	Cr (£)
			31/12/X6	Bal b/f	160

Discount allowed

Date	Description	Dr (£)	Date	Description	Cr (£)
31/12/X6	Bal b/f	575			

General expenses

Date	Description	Dr (£)	Date	Description	Cr (£)
31/12/X6	Bal b/f	2,250			

The general expenses balance needs to be adjusted for a closing accrual of £250

Commission received

Date	Description	Dr (£)	Date	Description	Cr (£)
			31/12/X6	Bal b/f	450

Commission received needs adjusting for income that was received by cheque of £200

Drawings

Date	Description	Dr (£)	Date	Description	Cr (£)
31/12/X6	Bal b/f	1,000			

There were no other accruals other than the accrual for general expenses detailed above.

(a) Using all the information given above and the balances given in the table below, enter the amounts into the appropriate trial balance columns for the accounts shown.

Extract from trial balance as at 31 December 20X6.

Account	£	Dr £	Cr £
Accruals			
Capital	25,000		
Wages and salaries	2,400		
Allowance for doubtful debt adjustment			
Receivables	11,000		
Drawings			
Entertainment expense	70		
Computer equipment at cost	2,600		
Computer equipment accumulated depreciation	1,200		
Commission received			
General expenses			
Discount allowed			

You are now ready to prepare the reconciliation of the purchases ledger control account (payables control account) to the purchases ledger.

The total of the balance on the purchases ledger control account is £11,500 compared to the total of the balances on the purchases ledger being £12,150. On investigation the following errors have been discovered:

1   A supplier account with a credit balance of £450 was duplicated in error.

2   A contra entry for £100 was made in the subsidiary (memorandum) ledger but was not entered into the control account in the general ledger.

3   A cash payment of £100 to a supplier was omitted from a supplier's individual account but was correctly posted in the general ledger.

4   The discounts received total of £200 was entered twice into the purchases ledger control account.

(b)   Use the following table to show the TWO adjustments required to the listing of the PURCHASES ledger. For the 'Add' and 'Deduct' columns, tick as appropriate.

Adjustment number	Amount (£)	Add	Deduct

(c)   Use the following table to show the TWO adjustments required to the PURCHASES LEDGER CONTROL account in the GENERAL ledger. For the 'Debit' and 'Credit' columns, tick as appropriate.

Adjustment number	Amount (£)	Debit	Credit

ACCOUNTING ADJUSTMENTS, SUSPENSE ACCOUNTS AND ERRORS

31   JACKSONS

You are working on the final accounts of Jacksons, a business with a year end of 31 May. A trial balance has been drawn up and a suspense account opened with a credit balance of £1,200. You need to make some corrections and adjustments for the year ended 31 May 20X1.

(a)   Record the adjustments needed on the extract from the extended trial balance to deal with the items below. (You will not need to enter adjustments on every line)

(i)   Entries need to be made for an irrecoverable debt of £220.

(ii)   A loan repayment of £1,600 has been made. The correct entry was made to the loan account but no other entries were made.

(iii)   No entries have been made for closing inventory for the year-end 31 May 20X1. Closing inventory has been valued at cost at £18,500. Included in this figure are some items costing £2,500 that will be sold for £1,700.

(iv)   The figures from the columns of the sales day book for 23 May have been totalled correctly as follows:

Sales column	£2,000
VAT column	£400
Total column	£2,400

The amounts have been posted as follows:

Cr Sales	£2,000
Cr VAT	£400
Dr Sales ledger control account	£2,000

Extract from extended trial balance

	Ledger balances		Adjustments	
	Dr £	Cr £	Dr £	Cr £
Allowance for doubtful debts		365		
Bank	4,300			
Closing inventory – statement of financial position				
Closing inventory – Statement of profit or loss				
Depreciation charge				
Irrecoverable debts				
Loan		4,000		
Loan interest	240			
Plant and machinery – accumulated depreciation		22,000		
Revenue		210,000		
Sales ledger control account	24,500			
Suspense		1,200		
VAT		5,600		

(b) The ledgers are ready to be closed off for the year ended 31 May 20X1. Show the correct entries to close off the loan interest account and include an appropriate narrative.

Account	Debit/Credit

32 PERCY

You are working on the final accounts of your friend Percy's business with a year-end of 31 December. A trial balance has been drawn up and a suspense account opened with a debit balance of £9,630. You need to make some corrections and adjustments for the year ended 31 December 20X1.

Record the journal entries needed in the general ledger to deal with the items below. You do not need to give narrative.

You should remove any incorrect entries, where appropriate, and post the correct entries.

(a) Two customers have been identified as having problems paying. Borrett Ltd owes £500 and hasn't made any payments for 3 months. Abbott & Co owes £715 and Percy has received notice of their liquidation.

Journal

	Dr £	Cr £

(b)   A payment of £880 for repairs to the company van has been made from the bank. The correct entry was made to the bank account but no other entries were made.

Journal

	Dr £	Cr £

(c)   No entries have been made for closing inventory for the year end 31 December 20X1. Closing inventory has been valued at cost at £33,821. Included in this figure are some items costing £5,211 that will be sold for £3,000.

Journal

	Dr £	Cr £

(d)   The figures from the columns of the purchases day book for 23 December have been totalled correctly as follows:

Purchases column	£25,000
VAT column	£4,375
Total column	£29,375

The amounts have been posted as follows:

Dr Purchases	£25,000
Cr VAT	£4,375
Cr Purchases ledger control account	£29,375

Journal

	Dr £	Cr £

33 HERMES DELIVERIES

Hermes Deliveries has a year end of 31 May. A trial balance has been drawn up and a suspense account opened with a credit balance of £12,525. You need to make some corrections and adjustments for the year ended 31 May 20X1.

Record the journal entries needed in the general ledger to deal with the items below. You do not need to give narrative.

You should remove any incorrect entries, where appropriate, and post the correct entries.

(a) A payment of £275 for printer cartridges and paper has been made from the bank. The correct entry was made to the bank, but no other entries were made.

Journal

	Dr £	Cr £

(b) No entries have been made for closing inventory, which has been valued at £34,962. After the year end, items which had originally been purchased for £2,741, were sold for £3,600.

Journal

	Dr £	Cr £

(c) Notice has been received of the liquidation of Kat Ltd. The sales ledger account shows a balance of £210.

Journal

	Dr £	Cr £

(d) The figures from the columns of the sales day book for 15 April have been totalled correctly as follows:

Sales column	£32,000
VAT column	£6,400
Total column	£38,400

The amounts have been posted as follows:

Dr Sales ledger control account	£38,400
Dr VAT	£6,400
Cr Revenue	£32,000

Journal

	Dr £	Cr £

34   EVANS AND CO

You are employed by Evans and Co, a bicycle manufacturer as their bookkeeper and they have asked you to create a trial balance. Below are the balances extracted from the main ledger at 31 May 20X0.

(a)   Enter the balances into the columns of the trial balance provided below. Total the two columns and enter an appropriate suspense account balance to ensure that the two totals agree.

	£	Debit	Credit
Capital	50,000		
Purchases	83,468		
Revenue	159,407		
Purchase returns	2,693		
Sales returns	3,090		
SLCA	25,642		
PLCA	31,007		
Drawings	25,500		
Machinery – Cost	45,900		
Machinery – Accumulated depreciation	15,925		
Rent and rates	15,600		
Light and heat	2,466		
Motor expenses	2,603		
Loan	12,500		
Interest paid	1,250		
Discounts received	400		
Irrecoverable debts	1,300		
Allowances for doubtful debts	2,572		
Salaries	77,921		
Bank overdraft	3,876		
Suspense			
Totals			

(b)   You are told of the following errors:

(i)   Drawings of £1,000 have been debited to the salaries account.

(ii)   The net column of the PDB has been overcast by £280.

(iii) The VAT column of the SDB has been undercast by £70.

(iv)   An amount of £3,175 paid for rent and rates has been debited to both the rent and rates account and the bank account.

(v)   An accrual for electricity at the year end of £340 has been correctly credited to the accruals account but no other entry has been made.

Prepare the entries to correct these errors using the blank journal below. Dates and narratives are not required.

		Dr £	Cr £
(i)			
(ii)			
(iii)			
(iv)			
(v)			

35 RACHEL EDMUNDSON

You are employed by Rachel Edmundson who is a florist. You are her bookkeeper and she has asked you to create a trial balance. Below are the balances extracted from the main ledger at 30 April 20X2.

(a) Enter the balances into the columns of the trial balance provided below. Total the two columns and enter an appropriate suspense account balance to ensure that the two totals agree.

	£	Debit	Credit
Accruals	4,820		
Prepayments	2,945		
Motor expenses	572		
Admin expenses	481		
Light and Heat	1,073		
Revenue	48,729		
Purchases	26,209		
SLCA	5,407		
PLCA	3,090		
Rent	45		
Purchase returns	306		
Discounts allowed	567		
Capital	10,000		
Loan	15,000		
Interest paid	750		
Drawings	4,770		
Motor vehicles – cost	19,000		
Motor vehicle – accumulated depreciation	2,043		
VAT control owing	2,995		
Wages	20,000		
Suspense account			
Totals			

(b)   Since the trial balance has been produced you have noticed a number of errors which are as follows:

(i)   Rachel put £5,000 into the business after receiving a large cheque as a Christmas present from her Gran. This has been put through the bank account but no other entries have been made.

(ii)   The Gross column of the SDB has been overcast by £385.

(iii)   The VAT column of the PDB has been undercast by £193.

(iv)   An amount of £4,500 paid for rent has been credited to both the rent account and the bank account.

(v)   An accrual for electricity at the year end of £1,356 has been correctly credited to the accruals account but no other entry has been made.

Prepare the entries to correct these errors using the blank journal below. Dates and narratives are not required.

		Dr £	Cr
(i)			
(ii)			
(iii)			
(iv)			
(v)			

36   BUSTER

You are working on the accounting records of Buster. A trial balance has been drawn up and a suspense account opened. You need to make some corrections and adjustments for the year ended 31 December 20X8. You may ignore VAT in this task.

Record the journal entries needed in the general ledger to deal with the items below.

You should remove any incorrect entries where appropriate and post the correct entries.

You do not need to give any narratives.

(a)   Motor expenses of £4,500 have been posted to the Motor Vehicles at Cost account in error. The other side of the entry is correct.

Journal

	Dr £	Cr £

(b)   Office sundries costing £16 were paid for by cash. Only the entry to the cash account was made.

Journal

	Dr £	Cr £

(c)   No entries have been made for closing inventory as at 31 December 20X8. It has been valued at a selling price of £227,184. The sales price has had 20% added onto its original cost.

Journal

	Dr £	Cr £

(d)   Discounts allowed of £1,270 have been posted as £1,720 on both sides of the entry.

Journal

	Dr £	Cr £

37 BRODIE

You are working on the accounting records of Brodie. A trial balance has been drawn up and a suspense account opened. You need to make some corrections and adjustments for the year ended 31 March 20X9. You may ignore VAT in this task.

Record the journal entries needed in the general ledger to deal with the items below.

You should remove any incorrect entries where appropriate and post the correct entries.

You do not need to give any narratives.

(a) The following adjustment for closing inventory has already been made in the accounts:

Dr Closing inventory (SFP) £10,000

Cr Closing inventory (SPL) £10,000

This adjustment was made without the knowledge that closing inventory of £2,000 can only be sold for 90% of the original cost.

You are required to remove the incorrect entry from the accounts and enter the revised closing inventory into the accounts.

Journal

	Dr £	Cr £

(b) Computer equipment is depreciated on a diminishing (reducing) balance basis at a rate of 10% per annum. As at 1 April 20X8 the balances of computer equipment at cost and the associated accumulated depreciation were £127,620 and £47,100 respectively. Enter the adjustment for the depreciation charge for the year ended 31 March 20X9. No additions or disposals were made during the year.

Journal

	Dr £	Cr £

(c) Following on from the information in part (b) -

What is the revised carrying amount of Computer Equipment as at 31 March 20X9?

....

(d) Brodie trades regularly with Carrie & Co. A contra entry for the value of £21,456 needs to be entered into the accounts for the year ended 31 March 20X9.

Journal

	Dr £	Cr £

THE EXTENDED TRIAL BALANCE

38 CARTERS

You have the following extended trial balance. The adjustments have already been correctly entered. You now need to extend the figures into the statement of profit or loss and statement of financial position columns. Make the columns balance by entering figures and a label in the correct places.

Extended trial balance

Ledger account	Ledger balances		Adjustments		Statement of profit or loss		Statement of financial position	
	Dr £	Cr £	Dr £	Cr £	Dr £	Cr £	Dr £	Cr £
Allowance for doubtful debts		1,300	600					
Allowance for doubtful debts adjustment				600				
Bank	28,380			500				
Capital		4,530						
Closing inventory			40,000	40,000				
Depreciation charge			20,500					
Office expenses	69,550			500				
Opening inventory	26,000							
Payroll expenses	31,150			150				
Purchases	188,000		900					
Purchases ledger control account		29,900						
Revenue		436,000						
Sales ledger control account	36,000							
Selling expenses	67,000							
Suspense		250	1,150	900				
VAT		9,800						
Vehicles at cost	62,000							
Vehicles accumulated depreciation		26,300		20,500				
	508,080	508,080	63,150	63,150				

39 GREENWOODS

You have the following extended trial balance. The adjustments have already been correctly entered. You now need to extend the figures into the statement of profit or loss and statement of financial position columns. Make the columns balance by entering figures and a label in the correct places.

Extended trial balance

Ledger account	Ledger balances		Adjustments		Statement of profit or loss		Statement of financial position	
	Dr £	Cr £	Dr £	Cr £	Dr £	Cr £	Dr £	Cr £
Accruals		2,300		425				
Advertising	1,800							
Bank	7,912		1,175					
Capital		40,000						
Closing inventory			6,590	6,590				
Depreciation charge			821					
Drawings	14,700							
Fixtures and fittings – accumulated depreciation		945		821				
Fixtures and fittings – cost	6,099							
Interest	345							
Light and heat	1,587		706					
Loan		10,000						
Opening inventory	5,215							
Prepayments	485		927	281				
Purchases	75,921							
PLCA		14,000						
Rent and rates	38,000			927				
Revenue		145,825						
SLCA	9,500			1,175				
VAT control account		11,453						
Wages	62,959							
	224,523	224,523	10,219	10,219				

40 WIDGETS LTD

You work for Widgets Ltd, a company that makes and sells parts for kitchen appliances. You have been provided with an ETB that has been started by the current bookkeeper. However, she is now on holiday and the owner of Widgets Ltd has asked that you create the adjustments and enter them onto the ETB to save time.

Make the appropriate entries in the adjustments column of the extended trial balance to take account of the following. The year end date is 31 December 20X5.

(a) The allowances for doubtful debts figure is to be adjusted to 2% of receivables.

(b) A credit note received from a supplier for goods returned was mislaid. It has since been found and has not yet been accounted for. It was for £2,000 net plus £400 VAT.

(c) Rent is payable yearly in advance. For the 12 months to 31/10/X5 the rent is £12,000, the prepayment bought down has been included in the ledger balance. For the 12 months to 31/10/X6 the rent is £15,000.

(d) Inventory is valued at cost at £14,890. However, there was a leak in the storage cupboard and £3,000 worth of items have been damaged and need to be written off.

(e) The electricity bill of £450 for the 3 months ended 31 January 20X6 was received and paid in February 20X6.

Extended trial balance

Ledger account	Ledger balances		Adjustments	
	Dr £	Cr £	Dr £	Cr £
Accruals		1,330		
Advertising	1,800			
Bank	7,912			
Capital		50,000		
Closing inventory				
Depreciation charge				
Drawings	14,700			
Fixtures and fittings – accumulated depreciation		945		
Fixtures and fittings – cost	6,099			
Irrecoverable debts	345			
Allowance for doubtful debt adjustment				
Electricity	1,587			
Loan	10,000			
Opening inventory	5,215			
Prepayment				
Allowance for doubtful debts		485		
Purchases	78,921			
Purchase returns				
PLCA		14,000		
Rent	25,000			
Revenue		145,825		
SLCA	9,500			
VAT control account		11,453		
Wages	62,959			
	224,038	224,038		

41   BINS 4 U LTD

You work for Bins 4 U Ltd, a company that makes and sells glasses. You have been provided with an ETB that has been started by the current bookkeeper. However, he has left unexpectedly and the owner of Bins 4 U Ltd has asked that you create the adjustments and enter them onto the ETB.

Make the appropriate entries in the adjustments column of the extended trial balance to take account of the following. The year end date is 31 May 20X7.

(a)   A credit note for a customer for goods returned was printed but never posted to the accounting system or to the customer. It was for £600 net plus £120 VAT.

(b)   After considering part (a), the allowance for doubtful debts is to be adjusted to 5% of the receivables balance.

(c)   Rent is payable yearly in advance. For the 12 months to 31/3/X7 the rent is £6,000, the prepayment brought forward has been included in the ledger balances. For the 12 months to 31/3/X8 the rent is going to be £7,500.

(d)   Inventory is valued at cost at £18,412. However, some items were sold after the year end for £2902 that originally cost £3,519.

(e)   The water bill for the 3 months ended 31 July 20X7 was received and paid in August 20X7. The bill was for £180.

Extended trial balance

Ledger account	Ledger balances		Adjustments	
	Dr	Cr	Dr	Cr
	£	£	£	£
Accruals		2,900		
Administration expenses	900			
Allowance for doubtful debts		1,040		
Bank overdraft		2,763		
Cash	246			
Capital		40,000		
Closing inventory				
Drawings	13,475			
Water	2,197			
Light and heat	2,018			
Loan		12,000		
Opening inventory	4,600			
Plant and machinery – accumulated depreciation		7,075		
Plant and machinery – cost	20,370			
Prepayments	1,200			
Purchases	100,159			
Rent	12,500			
Rates	8,500			
Salaries	46,376			
Revenue		151,606		
Sales returns				
SLCA	10,745			
Irrecoverable debts	850			
Allowance for doubtful debt adjustments				
VAT control account		6,752		
	224,136	224,136		

ETHICAL PRINCIPLES

42 APPROPRIATE ACTIONS

Read the statements below and assess whether these are appropriate actions to be taken or not.

	Appropriate action	Inappropriate action
You're working in the office on your own one evening and find that the payroll clerk has left the payroll filing cabinet unlocked. You want to know what your work colleague is paid so decide to take a look at the payroll file. No one will know so what's the harm?		
You recognise that your colleague has no idea what she is doing with the bank reconciliation so you offer some help and guidance as you have more than enough experience to lend a hand and provide some training.		
A new customer wants to place an order on credit for a substantial sum as a matter of urgency. The company normally follows very strict credit checks but a senior member of the team tells you that you don't need to bother on this occasion. They have told you it is fine not to follow normal company credit check procedures as they know one of the sales team.		

43 ACTING PROFESSIONALLY

Assess the following situations – are these examples of professional behaviour or not?

	Acting professionally	Not acting professionally
Checking social media websites during work time.		
Ensuring your knowledge is kept up to date by attending regular AAT branch meetings for continuing professional development.		
Realising you have made a mistake in a report you have just submitted to your manager and consequently informing them of your error.		
Walking into the office late and complaining about how much you wish it was still the weekend.		
Planning your work schedule to identify if there are going to be any issues in submitting the work for the set deadlines.		

44   ETHICAL PRINCIPLES 1

Match the act with the ethical principle that is being exercised.

Undertaking professional development	Objectivity
Not leaving work files unattended	Confidentiality
Not criticising colleagues on social media	Professional competence and due care
Reporting intimidating behaviour	Professional behaviour

45   ETHICAL PRINCIPLES 2

Match the definitions to the ethical principle

A member must be straightforward and honest in all professional and business relationships. It also implies fair dealing and truthfulness.	Professional behaviour
A member must not allow bias, conflict of interest or undue influence of others to override professional or business judgements.	Professional competence
A member has the knowledge and ability to discharge their responsibilities in accordance with current developments in practice, legislation and technique.	Confidentiality
A member must act diligently and in accordance with applicable technical and professional standards when providing professional services i.e. must not be negligent.	Objectivity
A member must act with discretion to keep information secret if it is not already in the public domain.	Integrity
A member should comply with relevant laws and regulations and should avoid any action that discredits the profession.	Due care

The following questions are not in the formal assessment style but are designed to develop your understanding of ethical principles.

46 ELLA

Ella, a professional accountant, was invited on a 'night out' with others from the accounts department. This became quite a boisterous evening and it ended with the Finance Director removing a sign from the front of a shop which he brought into the office the next day as a reminder of the good evening.

(a) State which fundamental ethical principle the Finance Director has breached.

(b) State what course of action Ella should take.

47 ROGER

Roger is an AAT member working for Lemon Ltd as an assistant to the management accountant. His finance director has asked him to post a journal to transfer £20,000, a material sum, out of maintenance costs and into non-current assets, thus boosting profit. Roger has checked the details and feels that there is no justification for the journal. Explain what Roger should do, highlighting both internal and external courses of action.

48 DILEMMA

Your boss has told you that there are going to be some redundancies in the company. You will not be affected, but he has named a number of people who will be, including a good friend of yours who is in the process of buying a holiday home in Cornwall. You know that your friend would not be able to afford the property if she were to lose her job and that she would pull out of the purchase if she knew about the redundancy plans. The news of the redundancies will not be made public for several weeks.

(a) State which fundamental ethical principle is primarily involved here.

(b) Assess the ethical argument that you should tell your friend about the redundancies on the grounds it could save her unnecessary financial problems and distress.

49 DAVINA

You are approached by your colleague Davina, who has received a complaint from a client (1) because she has not been able to produce a promised report on time (2). Davina says that this is because there is a new software system that she has not got to grips with yet (3), because she could not make it to the training event (4). Davina would like you to contact the client to tell them that there has been a problem with the system (5). She tells you more than you wish to know (6) about the background to the client's request. Office practice is for this type of report to be checked by a colleague before being sent out. Davina says that she has checked her own report, but asks you to sign it off without looking at it (7). You and Davina are friends and so you want to help (8). She also offers to buy you a drink (9) if you help. She also tells you not to tell anyone in case she gets into trouble (10).

(a) State which of the actions in the case study compromise integrity.

(b) State which of the actions in the case study compromise objectivity.

(c) State which of the actions in the case study compromise professional competence and due care.

(d) State which of the actions in the case study compromise confidentiality.

(e) State which of the actions in the case study compromise professional behaviour.

UNDERPINNING KNOWLEDGE

50   MULTIPLE CHOICE QUESTIONS

Choose ONE answer from each part.

1   Subsidiary sales ledger accounts are kept to

(a)   Summarise the total sales for the business

(b)   Show how much customers owe in total

(c)   Show how much each individual customer owes

(d)   Enable the production of individual supplier statements

2   Which one of the following concepts explains why we sometimes post prepayment adjustments in the accounts

(a)   The going concern concept

(b)   The prepayments concept

(c)   The accruals concept

(d)   The prudence concept

3   Inventory should be valued at the lower of:

(a)   Cost and net realisable value

(b)   Cost and carrying amount

(c)   Sales and net realisable value

(d)   Sales and carrying amount

4   Accounting for an expense that has been incurred but the cash has not yet been paid is accounting for:

(a)   A prepayment

(b)   An accrual

(c)   Depreciation

(d)   Deferred income

5   Irrecoverable debts are:

(a)   Amounts that are owed by customers that might not be received

(b)   Amounts that are owed by customers that have been received

(c)   Amounts that are owed by customers that will not be received

6   **Which of the following is the correct accounting equation?**

(a)   Non-current assets + Current assets = current liabilities + Long term liabilities

(b)   Assets + Liabilities = Capital – Profit + Drawings

(c)   Assets – Liabilities = Capital + Profit – Drawings

(d)   Capital = Profit – Drawings

7   **Prepayments are:**

(a)   An expense in the statement of profit or loss

(b)   An asset in the statement of financial position

(c)   Income in the statement of profit or loss

(d)   A liability in the statement of financial position

8   **A business buys a non-current asset on credit. Which elements of the accounting equation will be affected by this transaction?**

(a)   Assets only

(b)   Assets and liabilities only

(c)   Assets and capital only

(d)   Assets, liabilities and capital

9   Arty Partners has the following items of inventory at 31 December 20X9.

Component	Number held	Unit cost	Unit selling price
		£	£
A	100	3.00	3.60
B	150	2.50	2.70
C	20	4.50	4.20

What is the total value of inventory in the statement of financial position as at 31 December 20X9?

(a)   £855

(b)   £849

(c)   £759

(d)   £765

10   It is important to produce a trial balance prior to preparing the financial statements because:

(a)   it confirms the accuracy of the ledger accounts

(b)   it provides all the figures necessary to prepare the financial statements

(c)   it shows that the ledger accounts contain debit and credit entries of an equal value

(d)   it enables the accountant to calculate any adjustments required

11   A business with a large positive bank balance sends a cheque to a supplier of its inventory items, to settle part of the balance due to the supplier. Which elements of the accounting equation will be affected by this transaction?

(a)   Assets only

(b)   Assets and liabilities only

(c)   Assets and capital only

(d)   Assets, liabilities and capital

12   Which of the following is correct regarding the closing balance on a ledger account?

1   A credit balance exists where total credits exceed total debits

2   A credit balance exists where total debits exceed total credits

3   A debit balance exists where total debits exceed total credits

4   A debit balance exists where total credits exceed total debits

(a)   1 and 4 only

(b)   All of them

(c)   1 and 3 only

(d)   2 and 3 only

13   What is the missing word from the definition of asset provided?

'An asset is a resource _____ by the entity as a result of past events and from which future economic benefits are expected to flow to the entity.'

(a)   Owned

(b)   Used

(c)   Recognised

(d)   Controlled

14 Which of the following is the correct entry to record the purchase on credit of inventory intended for resale?

(a) Debit inventory, credit receivable

(b) Debit inventory, credit payable

(c) Debit purchases, credit payable

(d) Debit payable, credit purchases

15 The debit side of a trial balance totals £50 more than the credit side. This could be due to:

(a) a purchase of goods for £50 being omitted from the payables account

(b) a sale of goods for £50 being omitted from the receivables account

(c) an invoice of £25 for electricity being credited to the electricity account

(d) a receipt for £50 from a receivable being omitted from the cash book

16 The double entry system of bookkeeping normally results in which of the following balances on the ledger accounts?

(a) **Debit:** Assets and revenues **Credit:** Liabilities, capital and expenses

(b) **Debit:** Revenues, capital and liabilities **Credit:** Assets and expenses

(c) **Debit:** Assets and expenses **Credit:** Liabilities, capital and revenues

(d) **Debit:** Assets, expenses and capital **Credit:** Liabilities and revenues

17 Rent paid on 1 October 20X2 for the year to 30 September 20X3 was £1,200 and rent paid on 1 October 20X3 for the year to 30 September 20X4 was £1,600. Rent payable, as shown in the statement of profit or loss for the year ended 31 December 20X3 would be:

(a) £1,200

(b) £1,600

(c) £1,300

(d) £1,500

18 Which one of the following should be accounted for as capital expenditure?

(a) The cost of painting a building

(b) The replacement of windows in a building

(c) The purchase of a car by a garage for resale

(d) Legal fees incurred on the purchase of a building

19   An organisation's non-current assets register shows a carrying amount of £135,600. The non-current asset account in the general ledger shows a carrying amount of £125,600. The difference could be due to a disposed asset not having been deducted from the non-current assets register:

(a)   with disposal proceeds of £15,000 and a profit on disposal of £5,000

(b)   with disposal proceeds of £15,000 and a carrying amount of £5,000

(c)   with disposal proceeds of £15,000 and a loss on disposal of £5,000

(d)   with disposal proceeds of £5,000 and a carrying amount of £5,000

20   A non-current assets register is:

(a)   an alternative name for the non-current asset ledger account

(b)   a list of receivables and payables

(c)   a schedule of planned maintenance of non-current assets for use by the plant engineer

(d)   a schedule of the cost and other information about each individual non-current asset

Section 2

ANSWERS TO PRACTICE QUESTIONS

NON-CURRENT ASSETS REGISTER

1   SOUTHGATE TRADING

Description	Acquisition date	Cost £	Depreciation charges £	Carrying amount £	Funding method	Disposal proceeds	Disposal date
Computer equipment							
Server main office	30/09/X6	2,800.00			Cash		
Year end 31/03/X7			840.00	1,960.00			
Year end 31/03/X8			840.00	1,120.00			
Year end 31/03/X9			**840.00**	**280.00**			
HP printer 65438LKR	**28/03/X9**	**775.00**			**Credit**		
Year end 31/03/X9			**232.50**	**542.50**			
Motor vehicles							
AB08 DRF	01/04/X6	12,000.00			Cash		
Year end 31/03/X7			3,000.00	9,000.00			
Year end 31/03/X8			2,250.00	6,750.00			
Year end 31/03/X9			0	0		4,500.00	15/03/X9
AB 07 FRP	31/01/X8	9,600.00			Cash		
Year end 31/03/X8			2,400.00	7,200.00			
Year end 31/03/X9			**1,800.00**	**5,400.00**			

(d)   £660 (£250 + £410) – the cost of repainting the office is considered to be maintenance – revenue expenditure.

---

2   TK FABRICATIONS

Description	Acquisition date	Cost £	Depreciation charges £	Carrying amount £	Funding method	Disposal proceeds	Disposal date
Equipment							
Workshop fit out	17/07/X6	5,400.00			Cash		
Year end 31/01/X7			810.00	4,590.00			
Year end 31/01/X8			810.00	3,780.00			
Year end 31/01/X9			810.00	2,970.00			
Welding iron 289XP4	**28/01/X9**	**865.00**			**Credit**		
Year end 31/01/X9			**129.75**	**735.25**			
Motor vehicles							
PF07 THY	04/06/X6	13,500.00			Cash		
Year end 31/01/X7			3,375.00	10,125.00			
Year end 31/01/X8			2,531.25	7,593.75			
Year end 31/01/X9			0	0		**8,500.00**	**20/01/X9**
SR08 EKE	24/01/X8	7,300.00			Part-exchange		
Year end 31/01/X8			1,825.00	5,475.00			
Year end 31/01/X9			**1,368.75**	**4,106.25**			

3   BYTES TECHNOLOGY GROUP

Description	Acquisition date	Cost £	Depreciation charges £	Carrying amount £	Funding method	Disposal proceeds	Disposal date
Computer equipment							
Mainframe Server	17/07/X6	14,000.00			Cash		
Year end 31/03/X7			2,800.00	11,200.00			
Year end 31/03/X8			2,800.00	8,400.00			
Year end 31/03/X9			**2,800.00**	**5,600.00**			
Printer 180G92	**28/03/X9**	**560.00**			**Credit**		
Year end 31/03/X9			**112.00**	**448.00**			
Motor vehicles							
EJ09 TYZ	14/09/X6	9,000.00			Cash		
Year end 31/03/X7			2,700.00	6,300.00			
Year end 31/03/X8			1,890.00	4,410.00			
Year end 31/03/X9			0	0		**3,200.00**	**20/03/X9**
EA55 SAR	12/02/X8	10,000.00			Part-exchange		
Year end 31/03/X8			3,000.00	7,000.00			
Year end 31/03/X9			**2,100.00**	**4,900.00**			

(d)

	Tick
The location of the asset	✓

ACCOUNTING FOR NON-CURRENT ASSETS – ADDITIONS, DEPRECIATION AND DISPOSALS

4   VIVIENNE

Disposals

Computer equipment – cost	4,000	Computer equipment – accumulated depreciation	3,200
Statement of profit or loss	200	Computer equipment – cost	1,000
	4,200		4,200

Bank

Balance b/d	10,761	Computer equipment – cost	4,000
		Balance c/d	6,761
	10,761		10,761

5   A PARTNERSHIP

Vehicles at cost

Balance b/d	10,000	Balance c/d	17,500
Bank	7,500		
	17,500		17,500

Vehicles accumulated depreciation

Balance c/d	4,500	Balance b/d	3,000
		Depreciation charge	1,500
	4,500		4,500

Depreciation charge

Balance b/d	1,000	Statement of profit or loss	2,500
Vehicles accumulated depreciation	1,500		
	2,500		2,500

	Tick
A partner of the business	✓

6   SOLE TRADER

Vehicles at cost

Balance b/d	26,000	**Balance c/d**	**44,000**
Bank	18,000		
	44,000		44,000

Vehicles accumulated depreciation

Balance c/d	**8,800**	Balance b/d	6,500
		Depreciation charge	**2,300**
	8,800		**8,800**

Depreciation charge

Balance b/d	3,000	**Statement of profit or loss**	**5,300**
Vehicles accumulated depreciation	**2,300**		
	5,300		**5,300**

7   KATY'S CAKES

Equipment at cost

Balance b/d	6,200	**Balance c/d**	**14,700**
Bank	8,500		
	14,700		14,700

Equipment accumulated depreciation

Balance c/d	**3,180**	Balance b/d	1,900
		Depreciation charge – existing	**430**
		Depreciation charge – new	**850**
	3,180		**3,180**

Depreciation charge

Balance b/d	3,000	**Statement of profit or loss**	**4,280**
Accum. Dep'n – existing	**430**		
Accum. Dep'n – new	**850**		
	4,280		**4,280**

(d)

	Tick
The money spent on the purchase of non-current assets	✓

8 MILES 2 GO LIMITED

Narrative	Dr	Cr
Disposals	12,000.00	
Vehicles at cost		12,000.00
Vehicles accumulated depreciation	9,119.00	
Disposals		9,119.00
Vehicles at cost	15,250.00	
Motor vehicle expenses	210.00	
Disposals		3,800.00
Sundry payables		11,660.00
Totals	36,579.00	36,579.00

9 FLINT FARMS

(a)

Narrative	Dr	Cr
Disposals	32,000.00	
Vehicle at cost		32,000.00
Vehicles accumulated depreciation*	8,672.00	
Disposals		8,672.00
Vehicle at cost	40,800.00	
Insurance	2,500.00	
Disposals		8,500.00
Sundry payables		34,800.00
Totals	83,972.00	83,972.00

Key answer tips

The length of ownership of this vehicle is 2 years 11 months; therefore it was acquired on 18th September W7. The year end is 30th September and a full year's depreciation is charged in the year of acquisition with no charge in the year of disposal. This vehicle will be depreciated for year W7, W8 & W9 (it is disposed of in X0 therefore in accordance with the policy no depreciation will be charged in this year). Therefore three years of depreciation are charged at 10% diminishing (reducing) balance basis.

Year W7 £32,000 × 10% = £3,200

Year W8 £28,800 × 10% = £2,880

Year W9 £25,920 × 10% = £2,592

Accumulated depreciation £8,672

(b)

Rent	Revenue
Van	Capital
Installation of air conditioning	Capital
Repairing a window	Revenue

10   LEO LIGHTING

(a)   Year ended 31/12/X1 £20,000 × 10% = £2,000

Year ended 31/12/X2 (£20,000 – £2,000) × 10% = £1,800

Year ended 31/12/X3 (£20,000 – £2,000 – £1,800) × 10% = £1,620

Total accumulated depreciation (£2,000 + £1,800 + £1,620) = £5,420

(b)

Narrative	Dr	Cr
Disposals account	20,000	
Machinery cost account		20,000
Machinery accumulated depreciation account	5,420	
Disposals account		5,420
Bank	10,000	
VAT Control (20/120 × £10,000)		1,667
Disposals account (100/120 × £10,000)		8,333
Totals	35,420	35,420

Disposals

Machinery at cost	20,000	Machinery accumulated depreciation	5,420
		Bank	8,333
		Loss on disposal	6,247
	20,000		20,000

The profit or loss on disposal can also be calculated by comparing the sales proceeds to the carrying amount. The sales proceeds are £8,333 compared to a carrying amount of £14,580.

Therefore, a loss of £6,247 has been made.

11 FRED FARRIER

(a) £1,600

(£9,250 – £1,250)/5 years

(b) & (c)

Equipment at cost

Balance b/d	38,200		
Bank	9,250		
		Balance c/d	47,450
	47,450		47,450

Equipment accumulated depreciation

		Balance b/d	12,200
		Depreciation charges	1,600
Balance c/d	13,800		
	13,800		13,800

Depreciation charge

Balance b/d	2,300		
Accumulated depreciation (equipment)	1,600		
		Statement of profit or loss	3,900
	3,900		3,900

(d) £5,500

(e) £512

Tutorial note

The carrying amount is calculated by deducting the accumulated depreciation from the cost.

Cost – accumulated depreciation = carrying amount

Calculation of accumulated depreciation:

Depreciation charges for years 1 – 3

Year 1: £1,000 × 20%	£200
Year 2: (£1,000 – £200) × 20%	£160
Year 3: (£1,000 – £200 – £160) × 20%	£128
Accumulated depreciation	£488

Carrying amount = £512 (cost £1,000 – accumulated depreciation £488)

12   UNITS OF PRODUCTION METHOD

Machinery at cost

Bank	120,000	Balance c/d	120,000
	120,000		**120,000**

Machinery accumulated depreciation

Balance c/d	5,500	Depreciation charge	5,500
	5,500		**5,500**

Depreciation charge

Machinery accumulated depreciation	5,500	Statement of profit or loss	5,500
	5,500		**5,500**

Working for depreciation calculation:

(50,000 units/1,000,000 units) × (£120,000 – £10,000)

= £5,500

ACCOUNTING FOR ACCRUALS AND PREPAYMENTS OF INCOME AND EXPENSES

13   EXPENSES LEDGER ACCOUNTS (1)

Administration expenses

Bank	7,190	Reversal of accrued expenses	790
		Statement of profit or loss	4,600
		Prepaid expenses	1,800
	7,190		7,190

Selling expenses

Reversal of prepaid expenses	475	Statement of profit or loss	9,275
Bank	7,900		
Accrued expenses	900		
	9,275		9,275

Extract from trial balance as at 31 March 20X1.

Account	£	Dr £	Cr £
Accruals			900
Capital	6,000		6,000
Wages and salaries	850	850	
Selling expenses		9,275	
Drawings	11,000	11,000	
Administration expenses		4,600	
Interest received	70		70
Machinery at cost	5,600	5,600	
Machinery accumulated depreciation	4,200		4,200
Prepayments		1,800	

14 EXPENSES LEDGER ACCOUNTS (2)

Electricity expenses

Bank	10,539	Reversal of accrued expenses	2,815
		Statement of profit or loss	6,152
		Prepaid expenses	1,572
	10,539		10,539

Rental expenses

Reversal of prepaid expenses	6,250	Statement of profit or loss	75,000
Bank	62,500		
Accrued expenses	6,250		
	75,000		75,000

Extract from trial balance as at 31 March 20X6.

Account	£	Dr £	Cr £
Accruals			6,250
Accumulated depreciation – Office equipment	17,921		17,921
Depreciation charge	3,805	3,805	
Drawings	22,400	22,400	
Electricity		6,152	
Interest received	129		129
Office Equipment – cost	42,784	42,784	
Rental		75,000	
Stationery	2,800	2,800	
Prepayments		1,572	

15 EXPENSES LEDGER ACCOUNTS (3)

Telephone expenses

Bank	12,645	Reversal of accrued expenses	4,375
		Statement of profit or loss	6,844
		Prepaid expenses	1,426
	12,645		12,645

Rates expenses

Reversal of prepaid expenses	5,000	Statement of profit or loss	96,000
Bank	82,750		
Accrued expenses	8,250		
	96,000		96,000

Extract from trial balance as at 31 December 20X8

Account	£	Dr £	Cr £
Accruals			8,250
Accumulated depreciation – Machinery	15,437		15,437
Bank charges	2,897	2,897	
Capital	27,000		27,000
Discounts allowed	520	520	
Light and heat	4,000	4,000	
Machinery – cost	41,697	41,697	
Prepayments		1,426	
Rates		96,000	
Telephone		6,844	

16   INCOME AND EXPENSES LEDGER ACCOUNTS (1)

(a)   Complete the following statements:

On 01/04/X7, the commission receivable account shows a **debit** balance of **£3,200**. On 31/03/X8 the commission receivable account shows an adjustment for **accrued income** of **£2,800**.

(b)   Calculate the commission receivable for the year ended 31 March 20X8:

£22,400.

(c)   The bank summary for the year shows payments for telephone expenses of £1,896.

Update the telephone expense account for this, showing clearly the balance carried down.

Telephone expenses

Reversal of prepaid expenses	125		
Bank	1,896		
		Statement of profit or loss	2,021
	2,021		2,021

(d)   The amount to be transferred to the statement of profit or loss for telephone expenses will be **£110 greater** than the figure in (c).

Telephone expenses will show as a **debit** balance in the statement of profit or loss in the general ledger.

17   INCOME AND EXPENSES LEDGER ACCOUNTS (2)

(a)   Complete the following statements:

On 01/01/X8, the rental income account shows a **credit** balance of **£1,800**. On 31/12/X8 the rental income account shows an adjustment for **prepaid income** of **£2,000**.

(b)   Calculate the rental income for the year ended 31 December 20X8:

£17,800.

(c)   The bank summary for the year shows payments for office expenses of £2,600.

Update the telephone expense account for this, showing clearly the amount transferred to the statement of profit or loss.

Office expenses

Bank	2,600	Reversal of accrued expenses	120
		Statement of profit or loss	2,480
	2,600		2,600

(d)   The amount to be transferred to the statement of profit or loss for office expenses will be **£800 greater** than the figure in (c).

Office expenses will show as a **debit** balance in the statement of profit or loss in the general ledger.

18   COLETTE

(a)   **General expenses**

Date	Description	Dr	Date	Description	Cr
			1/1/20X8	Accrued expenses reversal	
					£1,000

(b)   On the 31st December 20X8 the general ledger account for general expenses shows a credit entry for prepaid expenses carried down of £750 .

(c)   £6,750.

19   MAIKI

(a)   **Sundry expenses**

Date	Description	Dr	Date	Description	Cr
1/4/20X6	Prepaid expenses reversal	£1,500			

(b)   On the 31st March 20X7 the general ledger account for sundry expenses shows a debit entry for accrued expenses carried down of £500 .

(c)   £13,500 .

20   RENT EXPENSE

(a)   Statement of profit or loss: £2,250

Prepayment: £600

Key answer tips

The financial year is 1 October 20X6 to 30 September 20X7. Out of the rental charge for 1 January – 31 December 20X6 three out of the total of twelve months relates to the financial year. Out of the rental charge for 1 January – 31 December 20X7 nine out of the total of twelve months relates to the financial year. The remaining three months of that rental charge have been prepaid as at the financial year end date 30 September 20X7.

Statement of profit or loss rental charge:

3/12 × £1,800	= £450
9/12 × £2,400	= £1,800
	———
Total rental charge	= £2,250
Prepayment:	
3/12 × £2,400	= £600

(b)

Accrued at 30 September 20X7	Charge to the statement of profit or loss year ended 30 September 20X7
£175	£2,650

Key answer tips

The financial year is 1 October 20X6 to 30 September 20X7. As at 1 October 20X6 there is an opening accrual for £200 – this relates to expense that occurred in the prior year but which will be paid in the current year. In accordance with the accruals concept the expense would have been recognised in the prior year when it was incurred and so it should not be recognised again when it is paid in the current year.

No electricity expense has been recognised for the month of September 20X7 therefore it needs to be accrued for. The accrual will be estimated based on the most recent bill which was for £525 for 3 months charge.

Statement of profit or loss electricity charge:

£2,650

£600 – £200 (opening accrual) + £800 + £750 + £525 + £175 (estimated closing accrual)

Accrual:

£175 (1/3 × £525)

(c)   **Extract** from trial balance as at 30 September 20X7.

Account	£	Dr £	Cr £
Accruals			175
Capital	100,000		100,000
Wages and salaries	25,000	25,000	
Rental expense		2,250	
Drawings	5,000	5,000	
Electricity expense		2,650	
Interest paid	950	950	
Computer equipment at cost	4,575	4,575	
Computer equipment accumulated depreciation	1,550		1,550
Prepayments		600	

21 RENTAL EXPENSES

(a) Calculate the value of the adjustment required for rental expenses as at 31 March 20X7.

£4,025 (Calculated as: (9/12 × £1,500) + £2,900)

(b) Update the rental expenses account.

Rental expenses

Prepaid expenses (reversal)	1,800	Prepaid expenses	4,025
Bank	10,550	Statement of profit or loss	8,325
	12,350		12,350

RECONCILIATIONS

22 BANK RECONCILIATION (1)

Adjustment	Amount £	Debit/Credit
Adjustment for (1)	82	Cr
Adjustment for (2)	90	Dr
Adjustment for (4)	1,750	Dr

Key answer tips

Cash book

Balance b/d	5,472	Adjustment (1)	82
Adjustment (2)	90		
Adjustment (4)	1,750		
		Balance c/d	7,230
	7,312		7,312

Balance of bank account	5,250
Uncleared lodgements	1,980
	7,230

23   BANK RECONCILIATION (2)

Adjustment	Amount £	Debit/Credit
Adjustment for (2)	106	Cr
Adjustment for (3)	350	Dr
Adjustment for (4)	1,645	Dr

Key answer tips

Cash book

Balance b/d	103	Adjustment (2)	106
Adjustment (3)	350		
Adjustment (4)	1,645		
		Balance c/d	1,992
	2,098		2,098

Balance of bank account	363
Uncleared lodgements	1,629
	1,992

24   BANK RECONCILIATION (3)

- – i, ii, iii
- – i, iii, v
- – **i, ii, iv**
- – iii, iv, v

25   PURCHASES LEDGER CONTROL ACCOUNT

	Add/Subtract	£
Total from list of balances		52,750
Adjustment for (a)	Subtract	8,370
Adjustment for (b)	Subtract	540
Adjustment for (c)	Add	750
Adjustment for (d)	Add	462
Adjustment for (e)	Add	1,902
Adjustment for (f)	Add	540
Revised total to agree with PLCA		47,494

26 PURCHASES LEDGER CONTROL ACCOUNT (2)

	Add/Subtract	£
Total from list of balances		132,589
Adjustment for (a)	Add	445
Adjustment for (b)	Subtract	4,340
Adjustment for (c)	Subtract	1,200
Adjustment for (d)	Subtract	132
Adjustment for (e)	Add	2,100
Adjustment for (f)	Add	120
Revised total to agree with PLCA		129,582

27 SALES LEDGER CONTROL ACCOUNT

	Add/Subtract	£
Total from list of balances		31,820
Adjustment for (a)	Subtract	73
Adjustment for (b)	Add	280
Adjustment for (c)	Subtract	5,542
Adjustment for (d)	Add	3,090
Adjustment for (e)	Add	935
Adjustment for (f)	Add	450
Revised total to agree with SLCA		30,960

28 SALES LEDGER CONTROL ACCOUNT (2)

	Add/Subtract	£
Total from list of balances		31,100
Adjustment for (a)	Add	65
Adjustment for (b)	Subtract	280
Adjustment for (c)	Subtract	1,170
Adjustment for (d)	Add	3,600
Adjustment for (e)	Subtract	99
Adjustment for (f)	Subtract	100
Revised total to agree with SLCA		33,116

29 ANDREAS

(a) **Extract** from trial balance as at 30 December 20X6.

Account	£	Dr £	Cr £
Bank		11,000	
Capital	24,198		24,198
Discounts received			300
Electricity		350	
Fixtures & fittings at cost	11,000	11,000	
Fixtures & fittings accumulated depreciation	2,400		2,400
Irrecoverable debt expense		1,987	
Misc. expense	2,600	2,600	
Prepaid expense		100	
Prepaid income			500
Rental income			3,000
Stationery	55	55	

(b)

Adjustment number	Amount (£)	Add	Deduct
1	157		✓
2	100		✓

(c)

Adjustment number	Amount (£)	Debit	Credit
2	100		✓
3	350		✓
4	200	✓	

30   KYLE

(a)   **Extract** from trial balance as at 31 December 20X6.

Account	£	Dr £	Cr £
Accruals			250
Capital	25,000		25,000
Wages and salaries	2,400	2,400	
Allowance for doubtful debt adjustment			160
Receivables	11,000	11,000	
Drawings		1,000	
Entertainment expense	70	70	
Computer equipment at cost	2,600	2,600	
Computer equipment accumulated depreciation	1,200		1,200
Commission received			650
General expenses		2,500	
Discount allowed		575	

(b)

Adjustment number	Amount (£)	Add	Deduct
1	450		✓
3	100		✓

(c)

Adjustment number	Amount (£)	Debit	Credit
2	100	✓	
4	200		✓

ACCOUNTING ADJUSTMENTS, SUSPENSE ACCOUNTS AND ERRORS

31   JACKSONS

(a)   **Extract** from extended trial balance

	Ledger balances		Adjustments	
	Dr £	Cr £	Dr £	Cr £
Allowance for doubtful debts		365		
Bank	4,300			1,600
Closing inventory – SoFP			17,700	
Closing inventory – SPL				17,700
Depreciation charge				
Irrecoverable debts			220	
Loan		4,000		
Loan interest	240			
Plant and machinery – accumulated depreciation		22,000		
Sales		210,000		
Sales ledger control account	24,500		400	220
Suspense		1,200	1,600	400
VAT		5,600		

(b)

Account	Debit/Credit
Statement of profit or loss	Debit
Loan interest	Credit
Transfer of loan interest charge for year to SPL	

32   PERCY

(a)   **Journal**

	Dr £	Cr £
Irrecoverable debt/Allowance for doubtful debt adjustment	500	
Allowance for doubtful debt		500
Irrecoverable debt	715	
Sales ledger control account		715

(b) **Journal**

	Dr £	Cr £
Motor repairs	880	
Suspense		880

(c) **Journal**

	Dr £	Cr £
Closing inventory – statement of financial position	31,610	
Closing inventory – statement of profit or loss		31,610

Tutorial note

Inventory is valued at the lower of cost and net realisable value. The original inventory value of £33,821 needs to be adjusted as some inventory has been identified in which its cost exceeds its net realisable value. Therefore the cost of £5,211 needs to be removed and revalued at the lower NRV of £3,000.

33,821 – 5,211 + 3,000 = 31,610.

(d) **Journal**

	Dr £	Cr £
VAT	4,375	
Suspense		4,375
VAT	4,375	
Suspense		4,375

Key answer tip

Suspense account

Balance b/d	9,630	Motor repairs	880
		VAT	4,375
		VAT	4,375
	9,630		9,630

33 HERMES DELIVERIES

Journal

	Dr £	Cr £
Stationery	275	
Suspense		275

Journal

	Dr £	Cr £
Closing inventory – SoFP	34,962	
Closing inventory – SPL		34,962

Journal

	Dr £	Cr £
Irrecoverable debt	210	
Sales ledger control account		210

Journal

	Dr £	Cr £
Suspense	6,400	
VAT		6,400
Suspense	6,400	
VAT		6,400

Key answer tip

Suspense account

VAT	6,400	Balance b/d	12,525
VAT	6,400	Stationery	275
	12,800		12,800

34 EVANS AND CO

(a)

	£	Debit	Credit
Capital	50,000		50,000
Purchases	83,468	83,468	
Revenue	159,407		159,407
Purchase returns	2,693		2,693
Sales returns	3,090	3,090	
SLCA	25,642	25,642	
PLCA	31,007		31,007
Drawings	25,500	25,500	
Machinery – Cost	45,900	45,900	
Machinery – Accumulated depreciation	15,925		15,925
Rent and rates	15,600	15,600	
Light and heat	2,466	2,466	
Motor expenses	2,603	2,603	
Loan	12,500		12,500
Interest	1,250	1,250	
Discounts received	400		400
Irrecoverable debts	1,300	1,300	
Allowances for doubtful debts	2,572		2,572
Salaries	77,921	77,921	
Bank overdraft	3,876		3,876
Suspense			**6,360**
Totals		284,740	284,740

(b)

		Dr £	Cr
(i)	Drawings	1,000	
	Salaries		1,000
(ii)	Suspense	280	
	Purchases		280
(iii)	Suspense	70	
	VAT		70
(iv)	Suspense	3,175	
	Bank		3,175
	Suspense	3,175	
	Bank		3,175
(v)	Electricity	340	
	Suspense		340

35 RACHEL EDMUNDSON

(a)

	£	Debit	Credit
Accruals	4,820		4,820
Prepayments	2,945	2,945	
Motor expenses	572	572	
Administration expenses	481	481	
Light and heat	1,073	1,073	
Revenue	48,729		48,729
Purchases	26,209	26,209	
SLCA	5,407	5,407	
PLCA	3,090		3,090
Rent	45	45	
Purchase returns	306		306
Discounts allowed	567	567	
Capital	10,000		10,000
Loan	15,000		15,000
Interest paid	750	750	
Drawings	4,770	4,770	
Motor vehicles – cost	19,000	19,000	
Motor vehicle – accumulated depreciation	2,043		2,043
VAT control	2,995		2,995
Wages	20,000	20,000	
Suspense account		**5,164**	
Totals		86,983	86,983

(b)

		Dr £	Cr £
(i)	Suspense	5,000	
	Capital		5,000
(ii)	Suspense	385	
	Sales ledger control account		385
(iii)	VAT	193	
	Suspense		193
(iv)	Rent	4,500	
	Suspense		4,500
	Rent	4,500	
	Suspense		4,500
(v)	Electricity	1,356	
	Suspense		1,356

36 BUSTER

(a) **Journal**

	Dr £	Cr £
Motor expenses	4,500	
Motor vehicles at cost		4,500

(b) **Journal**

	Dr £	Cr £
Office sundries	16	
Suspense		16

(c)   **Journal**

	Dr £	Cr £
Closing inventory – statement of financial position	189,320	
Closing inventory – statement of profit or loss		189,320

Tutorial note

Inventory is valued at the lower of cost and net realisable value. The selling price is given as £227,184. To get to the selling price, 20% of the value of the cost is added to the cost. The cost of £189,320 has been calculated by dividing the selling price by 120 and then multiplying by 100.

(227,184/120) × 100 = 189,320

The value of closing inventory, in accordance with IAS 2 is £189,320.

(d)   **Journal**

	Dr £	Cr £
Receivables	1,720	
Discounts allowed		1,720
Discounts allowed	1,270	
Receivables		1,270

37 BRODIE

(a) **Journal**

	Dr £	Cr £
Closing inventory - SPL	10,000	
Closing inventory – SoFP		10,000
Closing inventory – SoFP	9,800	
Closing inventory – SPL		9,800

(b) **Journal**

	Dr £	Cr £
Depreciation expense	8,052	
Provision for accumulated depreciation		8,052

(c) **The revised carrying amount as at 31 March 20X9 is £72,468**

Key answer tip

Carrying amount as at 1 April 20X8	£80,520
Less: Depreciation charge for the year to 31 March 20X9	£8,052
Carrying amount as at 31 March 20X9	£72,468

(d) **Journal**

	Dr £	Cr £
Payables	21,456	
Receivables		21,456

THE EXTENDED TRIAL BALANCE

38   CARTERS

Extended trial balance

Ledger account	Ledger balances		Adjustments		Statement of profit or loss		Statement of financial position	
	Dr £	Cr £	Dr £	Cr £	Dr £	Cr £	Dr £	Cr £
Allowance for doubtful debts		1,300	600					700
Allowance for doubtful debts adjustment				600		600		
Bank	28,380			500			27,880	
Capital		4,530						4,530
Closing inventory			40,000	40,000		40,000	40,000	
Depreciation charge			20,500		20,500			
Office expenses	69,550			500	69,050			
Opening inventory	26,000				26,000			
Payroll expenses	31,150			150	31,000			
Purchases	188,000			900	188,900			
Purchases ledger control account		29,900						29,900
Revenue		436,000				436,000		
Sales ledger control account	36,000						36,000	
Selling expenses	67,000				67,000			
Suspense		250	1,150	900				
VAT		9,800						9,800
Vehicles at cost	62,000						62,000	
Vehicles accumulated depreciation		26,300		20,500				46,800
Net profit					74,150			74,150
	508,080	508,080	63,150	63,150	476,600	476,600	165,880	165,880

39   GREENWOODS

Extended trial balance

Ledger account	Ledger balances		Adjustments		Statement of profit or loss		Statement of financial position	
	Dr £	Cr £	Dr £	Cr £	Dr £	Cr £	Dr £	Cr £
Accruals		2,300		425				2,725
Advertising	1,800				1,800			
Bank	7,912		1,175				9,087	
Capital		40,000						40,000
Closing inventory			6,590	6,590		6,590	6,590	
Depreciation charge			821		821			
Drawings	14,700						14,700	
Fixtures and fittings – accumulated depreciation		945		821				1,766
Fixtures and fittings – cost	6,099						6,099	
Interest	345				345			
Light and heat	1,587		706		2,293			
Loan	.	10,000						10,000
Opening inventory	5,215				5,215			
Prepayments	485		927	281			1,131	
Purchases	75,921				75,921			
PLCA		14,000						14,000
Rent and rates	38,000			927	37,073			
Revenue		145,825				145,825		
SLCA	9,500			1,175			8,325	
VAT control account		11,453						11,453
Wages	62,959				62,959			
Loss						34,012	34,012	
	224,523	224,523	10,219	10,219	186,427	186,427	79,944	79,944

40   WIDGETS LTD

Extended trial balance

Ledger account	Ledger balances		Adjustments	
	Dr £	Cr £	Dr £	Cr £
Accruals		1,330		300
Advertising	1,800			
Bank	7,912			
Capital		50,000		
Closing inventory			11,890	11,890
Depreciation charge				
Drawings	14,700			
Fixtures and fittings – accumulated depreciation		945		
Fixtures and fittings – cost	6,099			
Irrecoverable debts	345			
Allowance for doubtful debt adjustment				295
Electricity	1,587		300	
Loan	10,000			
Opening inventory	5,215			
Prepayment			12,500	
Allowance for doubtful debts		485	295	
Purchases	78,921			
Purchase returns				2,000
PLCA		14,000	2,400	
Rent	25,000			12,500
Revenue		145,825		
SLCA	9,500			
VAT control account		11,453		400
Wages	62,959			
	224,038	224,038	27,385	27,385

Key answer tips

(a)   SLCA 9,500 × 2% = 190. Allowance currently 485, therefore debit with £295 to make it equal £190

(c)   The prepayment for the year end is 10/12 × 15,000 = 12,500. For November and December X5 = 2/12 × 15,000 = 2,500. Total rental charge for the year = (10/12 × 12,000) + 2,500 = £12,500

(e)   Accrual for November and December. 2/3 × 450 = £300

41 BINS 4 U LTD

Extended trial balance

Ledger account	Ledger balances		Adjustments	
	Dr £	Cr £	Dr £	Cr £
Accruals		2,900		60
Admin expenses	900			
Allowance for doubtful debts		1,040	539	
Bank overdraft		2,763		
Cash	246			
Capital		40,000		
Closing inventory			17,795	17,795
Drawings	13,475			
Water	2,197		60	
Light and heat	2,018			
Loan		12,000		
Opening inventory	4,600			
Plant and machinery – accumulated depreciation		7,075		
Plant and machinery – cost	20,370			
Prepayments	1,200		6,250	
Purchases	100,159			
Rent	12,500			6,250
Rates	8,500			
Salaries	46,376			
Revenue		151,606		
Sales returns			600	
SLCA	10,745			720
Irrecoverable debts	850			
Allowance for doubtful debt adjustment				539
VAT control account		6,752	120	
	224,136	224,136	25,364	25,364

Key answer tips

(b) SLCA 10,745 − 720 = 10,025 × 5% = 501. Provision currently 1,040, therefore 539 needed to reduce provision

(c) The prepayment for rent is 7,500 × 10/12 = 6,250

(e) Accrue 1/3 × £180

ETHICAL PRINCIPLES

42   APPROPRIATE ACTIONS

	Appropriate action	Inappropriate action
You're working in the office on your own one evening and find that the payroll clerk has left the payroll filing cabinet unlocked. You want to know what your work colleague is paid so decide to take a look at the payroll file. No one will know so what's the harm?		x
You recognise that your colleague has no idea what she is doing with the bank reconciliation so you offer some help and guidance as you have more than enough experience to lend a hand and provide some training.	x	
A new customer wants to place an order on credit for a substantial sum as a matter of urgency. The company normally follows very strict credit checks but a senior member of the team tells you that you don't need to bother on this occasion. They have told you it is fine not to follow normal company credit check procedures as they know one of the sales team.		x

43   ACTING PROFESSIONALLY

	Acting professionally	Not acting professionally
Checking social media websites during work time.		x
Ensuring your knowledge is kept up to date by attending regular AAT branch meetings for continuing professional development.	x	
Realising you have made a mistake in a report you have just submitted to your manager and consequently informing them of your error.	x	
Walking into the office late and complaining about how much you wish it was still the weekend.		x
Planning your work schedule to identify if there are going to be any issues in submitting the work for the set deadlines.	x	

44 ETHICAL PRINCIPLES 1

Match the act with the ethical principle that is being exercised.

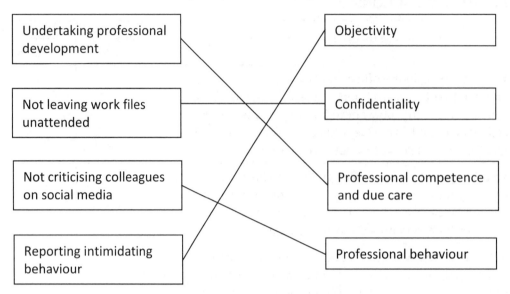

45 ETHICAL PRINCIPLES 2

Match the definitions to the ethical principle.

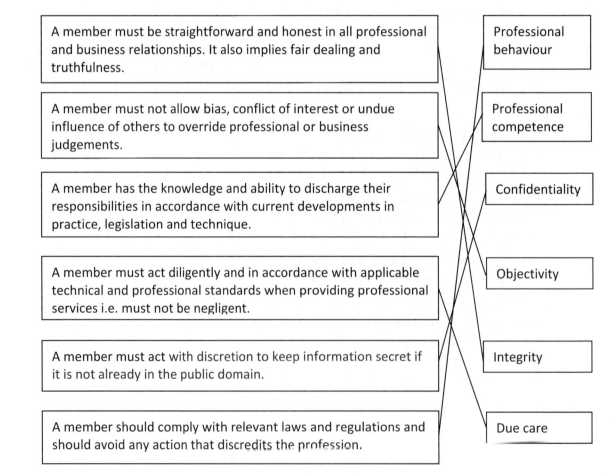

46 ELLA

(a) This situation displays a breach of Professional Behaviour.

(b) Bella should suggest to the Finance Director that he should replace the sign, and possibly discuss the matter with the Managing Director.

47 ROGER

Appropriate responses include the following:

Internal action

- Discuss the matter with the Finance Director to see if there is a valid case for posting this journal. From the information given, this seems unlikely.

External action

If the FD refuses to change the request and Roger still feels uncomfortable, then he could:

- go to the company's auditors to discuss the matter
- seek guidance from the AAT Ultimately if the situation is not resolved, then he should consider resigning.

Note: The wrong answer here is to suggest that he should post the journal without question as the Finance director is his senior. This is not an appropriate action.

48 DILEMMA

(a) Confidentiality.

(b) You should not tell your friend about the redundancies as to do so would breach confidentiality.

49 DAVINA

(a) Integrity – When you are asked to contact the client to tell them that there has been a problem with the system, (5) you are, in effect, being asked to tell a lie. At the very least you would be being reckless with the truth of having checked it if you sign it off without looking at it (7).

(b) Objectivity – It may be a small inducement, but it is an inducement when Davina says there is a drink in it for you if you help (9). The fact that you and Davina are friends and so you want to help (8) might indicate that you are being influenced in your decision- making by familiarity.

(c) Professional Competence and Due Care – When Davina says she has not been able to produce a promised report on time (2), it is clear that she is not professionally competent, which is reinforced by the fact that she is not able to operate the new software system that she has not got to grips with yet (3).

(d) Confidentiality – Generally, you should not be party to more than you wish to know about the background to the client's request (6), but then there can be a duty to disclose to a regulatory body when she tells you not to tell anyone in case she gets into trouble (10).

(e) Professional Behaviour – There is normally an appropriate way in which a complaint from a client (1) should be dealt with, while there is a continuing duty to develop, not only core skills, but those needed to work effectively for clients. Davina has compromised this when she could not make it to the training event (4).

UNDERPINNING KNOWLEDGE

50 MULTIPLE CHOICE QUESTIONS

1   (c)

2   (c)

3   (a)

4   (b)

5   (c)

6   (c)

7   (b)

8   (b)

9   (c)

10   (c)

11   (b)

12   (c)

13   (d)

14   (c)

15   (a)

16   (c)

17   (c)

The year to 31 December 20X3 includes 9 months (out of a total of 12 months) of the rent for the year to 30 September 20X3 and 3 months (out of a total of 12 months) of the rent for the year to 30 September 20X4: $(9/12 \times £1,200) + (3/12 \times £1,600) = £1,300$.

18   (d)

19   (a)

The difference between the two records is £10,000. The disposed asset must have had a carrying amount of this amount.

20   (d)

Section 3

MOCK ASSESSMENT QUESTIONS

TASK 1.1 (21 MARKS)

This task is about non-current assets.

You are an accounting technician working for Minn and Jones a firm of Chartered Certified Accountants. You are working on the non-current asset register of Oscar Office Supplies.

The following is an extract from purchase invoice received by Oscar Office Supplies:

To Oscar Office Supplies		**Invoice No: 791**
Spring Lane Business Centre		
Spring Lane		Computer Supplies
Essex		High Street
E121 3EX		Loughborough
		L017 3QE
		30 June X9
	£	
Canonfire laser printer (1)	1,750.00	
Delivery	20.00	
Printer cartridges (2)	70.00	
	_____	
	1,840.00	
VAT @ 20%	368.00	
	_____	
	£2,208.00	
	_____	

The following relates to the sale of a vehicle:

Registration number	MN 07 JON
Date of sale	30/09/X9
Selling price excluding VAT (sales tax)	£5,000

- Oscars has a policy of capitalising expenditure over £1,000.

- Vehicles are depreciated at 20% on a reducing balance basis.

- Computer equipment is depreciated at 30% on a straight line basis.

- Non-current assets are depreciated in the year of acquisition but not in the year of disposal.

Record the following information in the non-current asset register. (18 marks)

(a) **Any acquisitions during year ended X9**

(b) **Any disposals during year ended X9**

(c) **Depreciation for year ended X9**

Non-current assets Register

Description	Acquisition date	Cost	Deprecia-tion	CV	Funding source	Disposal proceeds	Disposal date
Computer equipment							
Computer network	30/9/X7	3,000.00			Cash		
Y/E 31/12/X7			900.00	2,100.00			
Y/E 31/12/X8			900.00	1,200.00			
Y/E 31/12/X9							
Laser printer	30/6/X9						
Y/E 31/12/X9							
Motor vehicles							
MN 07 JON	1/4/X7	21,000.00					
Y/E 31/12/X7			4,200.00	16,800.00			
Y/E 31/12/X8			3,360.00	13,440.00			
Y/E 30/12/X9							
MN 08 JON	1/1/X8	15,000.00			PT EX		
31/12/X8			3,000.00	12,000.00			
31/12/X9							

(d) **Who would be the most appropriate person to authorise capital expenditure? (1 mark)**

Bank manager	Office junior	Accounts payable clerk	Director of the business

(e) **Match the correct definitions on the right to the terms 'capital expenditure' and 'revenue expenditure' on the left. (2 marks)**

Capital expenditure		expenditure on non-current assets or on the improvement of non-current assets.

Revenue expenditure		amount of money spent by a business or organisation on general operating costs such as rent, insurance, heating, maintenance etc.

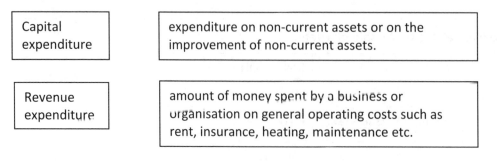

TASK 1.2 (17 MARKS)

This task is about ledger accounting for non-current assets.

You are working on the accounts of a partnership and are dealing with the acquisition and depreciation of motor vehicles.

- A new commercial vehicle has been acquired and VAT can be reclaimed on this vehicle. The vehicle was paid for by cheque.

- The cost of the vehicle including VAT was £12,000.

- The residual value (ex VAT) is expected to be £2,500.

- The depreciation policy for vehicles is 25% per annum on a straight line basis.

- Depreciation has already been entered into the accounts on existing vehicles.

Make the following entries: (12 marks)

(a) Purchase of the new vehicle.

(b) Depreciation on the vehicle acquired.

(c) Balance off the accounts and show any transfers to the statement of profit or loss.

Vehicles at cost			
	£		£
Bal b/d	28,500		

Accumulated depreciation			
	£		£
		Bal b/d	14,250

Depreciation charge			
	£		£
Bal b/d	7,125		

A business sold an item of equipment for cash proceeds of £4,000. The business made a profit on disposal of £500. The accumulated depreciation at the date of disposal was £2,000.

(d)   What was the original cost? (1 mark)

(e)   What is the accounting entry to record the disposal proceeds? (2 marks)

Account	Debit £	Credit £

(f)   What is the accounting entry to remove the accumulated depreciation? (2 marks)

Account	Debit £	Credit £

TASK 1.3 (19 MARKS)

This task is about ledger accounting, including accruals and prepayments, and applying ethical principles.

You are working on the final accounts of a business for year ended 31/12/X9.

You have the following information. The figures below are net of VAT.

Balance at	1/1/X9
Accrued administration expenses	£1,000
Prepaid selling expenses	£600

The bank summary for the year shows payments for administration expenses of £7,750 which included £1,500 for quarter ended 31/3/Y0.

(a)   Prepare the administration expenses account for year ended 31/12/X9. Close off the account, showing the charge to the statement of profit or loss for the year: (5 marks)

Administration expenses

Date	Account name	£	Date	Account name	£

The bank summary for the year shows selling expenses of £10,800 and selling expenses accrued are £275.

(b) Prepare the selling expenses account for year ended 31/12/X9. Close off the account showing the charge to the statement of profit or loss for the year: **(5 marks)**

Selling expenses

Date	Account name	£	Date	Account name	£

(c) Taking into account the information that follows, complete the statements:

You now find out that there is an unpaid invoice of £1,600 for some secretarial work for the 4 months beginning 1/10/X9. Secretarial work is classified as administration expenses.

The amount to be transferred to the statement of profit or loss for administration expenses will be £_____ (greater/less?) than the figure in (a).

Admin expenses will show as a _____ (debit/credit?) in the profit or loss account in the general ledger. **(2 marks)**

(d) Using the figures from your answers in (a) and (b) as well as balances given, complete the trial balance extract below as of 31st December 20X9. **(4 marks)**

Account	£	Dr	Cr
Revenue	9,690		
Discounts allowed	150		
SLCA	4,380		
Bank overdraft	350		
Accruals			
Prepayments			
Administration			
Selling expenses			

(e) Vernon, a member in practice, performs bookkeeping services for both Yen Ltd and Piston Ltd. The two companies are in dispute about a series of purchases that Yen Ltd made from Piston Ltd. Identify which fundamental ethical principles are threatened here from the options below. **(3 marks)**

A   Objectivity and confidentiality

B   Integrity and professional behaviour

C   Confidentiality and professional competence

TASK 1.4 (23 MARKS)

This task is about accounting adjustments and journals.

You are working on the preparation of a series of journal entries in preparation of a set of final accounts.

A trial balance has been prepared and a suspense account has been opened with a debit balance of £2,220. You need to make some adjustments to eliminate the suspense account and other journals for adjustments are required:

(a) **Entries need to be made to write off an irrecoverable debt of £675.**

Journal	Dr	Cr

(b) **A loan repayment of £1,500 has been entered in the cash book but no other entry was made:**

Journal	Dr	Cr

(c) **No entries have yet been made for closing inventory. It has been valued at cost £26,875, included in this figure is inventory that cost £1,875, but will be sold for £1,250:**

Journal	Dr	Cr

(d) The figures on the purchase of a non-current asset (tools and equipment) were as follows:

Cost   £1,800.00

VAT   £360.00
          ─────────

        £2,160.00
        ─────────

This had been posted as:

Tools and equipment	Dr	1,800.00
VAT	Cr	360.00
Bank	Cr	2,160.00

Journal	Dr	Cr

(e) You are now working on extending the trial balance for the adjustments you have dealt with in the journal entries prepared in Task 1.5 parts (a) – (d).

Record these adjustments and extend the Trial Balance for each item dealt with in the journals. Please note: this is a trial balance extract, not a complete trial balance.

	Ledger balances		Adjustments	
	Dr	Cr	Dr	Cr
Allowance for doubtful debts		625		
Bank	5,500			
Closing inventory (SFP)				
Closing inventory (SPL)				
Depreciation	3,750			
Irrecoverable debts				
Loan		10,000		
Loan Interest	500			
Accumulated depn plant and machinery		22,750		
Revenue		255,500		
Sales ledger control	29,550			
Suspense	2,220			
VAT account		5,400		

TASK 1.5 (20 MARKS)

This task is about period end routines, using accounting records and the extended trial balance.

(a)   You are working on reconciling the bank.

The following differences have been identified when comparing the cash book with the bank statements.

(1)   Bank interest paid £150, had not been entered in the cash book.

(2)   A cheque paid for £985 had been entered in the cash book as £958.

(3)   Cheques totalling £3,750 paid into the bank are not showing on the statement.

(4)   A BACS receipt of £3,550 from a customer has not been entered in the cash book.

(5)   Cheques drawn for £2,770, entered in the cash book are not showing on the bank statement.

Using the table below show the adjustments required to update the cash book: (4 marks)

Adjustment	Amount £	Debit	Credit
		(✓ as appropriate)	
(i)			
(ii)			
(iii)			

(b)   **Subsidiary purchases ledger accounts are kept to: (tick the appropriate answer) (1 mark)**

Summarise the total purchases	
Show how much suppliers owe in total	
Show much is owed to individual suppliers	
Enable the preparation of customer statements	

A Purchases Ledger Control account will show at any time in an accounting period: (tick appropriate answer) (1 mark)

How much each individual payable owes	
How much is owed in total to credit suppliers	
How much the total purchases have been in the period	
How many customers' accounts are overdue	

(c) You are now working on the final accounts of a sole trader.

The adjustments have already been made to the ETB.

Extend the figures to the statement of profit or loss and statement of financial position. (14 marks)

	Ledger balances		Adjustments		Statement of profit or loss		Statement of fin. pos	
	Dr	Cr	Dr	Cr	Dr	Cr	Dr	Cr
Capital		50,000						
Bank loan		10,000						
Non-current assets (Cost)	85,400							
Opening inventory	2,250							
Closing inventory			2,100	2,100				
Bank	3,125							
Cash	375							
Irrecoverable debts	600							
Allowance for doubtful debts		875						
Depreciation	15,875							
Sales ledger control	5,500							
Purchase ledger control		3,750						
Revenue		118,750						
Purchases	45,625							
Motor expenses	4,875		125					
Insurance	1,875			375				
Office expenses	1,125		250					
Wages	17,500		125					
Drawings	30,750							
Accumulated depreciation		31,750						
Accruals				250				
Prepayments			375					
Suspense	250			250				
Profit/Loss								
	£215,125	£215,125	£2,975	£2,975				

Section 4

MOCK ASSESSMENT ANSWERS

TASK 1.1

Non-current assets register (a – c)

Description	Acquisition date	Cost	Deprecia-tion	CV	Funding source	Disposal proceeds	Disposal date
Computer equipment							
Computer network	30/9/X7	3,000.00			Cash		
Y/E 31/12/X7			900.00	2,100.00			
Y/E 31/12/X8			900.00	1,200.00			
Y/E 31/12/X9			900.00	300.00			
Laser printer	30/6/X9	1,770.00			Credit		
Y/E 31/12/X9			531.00	1,239.00			
Motor vehicles							
MN 07 JON	1/4/X7	21,000.00					
Y/E 31/12/X7			4,200.00	16,800.00			
Y/E 31/12/X8			3,360.00	13,440.00			
Y/E 30/12/X9			0	0		5,000.00	30/09/X9
MN 08 JON	1/1/X8	15,000.00			PT EX		
31/12/X8			3,000.00	12,000.00			
31/12/X9			2,400.00	9,600.00			

(d)

Director
of the
business

(e)

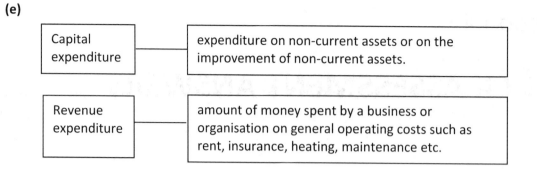

Capital expenditure	expenditure on non-current assets or on the improvement of non-current assets.
Revenue expenditure	amount of money spent by a business or organisation on general operating costs such as rent, insurance, heating, maintenance etc.

TASK 1.2

(a – c)

Vehicles at cost			
	£		£
Bal b/d	28,500	Bal c/d	38,500
Bank	10,000		
	38,500		38,500

Accumulated depreciation			
	£		£
Bal c/d	16,125	Bal b/d	14,250
		Depreciation charge	1,875
	16,125		16,125

Depreciation charge			
	£		£
Bal b/d	7,125	Statement of profit or loss	9,000
Accumulated depreciation	1,875		
	9,000		9,000

(d)

£5,500

Workings:

If a profit was made on disposal of £500 and the proceeds were £4,000 the carrying amount must have been £3,500. Accumulated depreciation at the date of disposal was £2,000 and so the original cost was £5,500 as cost less accumulated depreciation equals carrying amount.

(e)

Account	Debit £	Credit £
Bank	4,000	
Disposals		4,000

(f)

Account	Debit £	Credit £
Equipment – accumulated depreciation	2,000	
Disposals		2,000

TASK 1.3

(a)

Administration expenses

Date	Account name	£	Date	Account name	£
31/12/X9	Bank	7,750	1/1/X9	Reversal of accrued expenses	1,000
			31/12/X9	Prepaid expenses	1,500
			31/12/X9	Statement of profit or loss	5,250
		7,750			7,750

(b)

Selling expenses

Date	Account name	£	Date	Account name	£
1/1/X9	Reversal of prepaid expenses	600	31/12/X9	Statement of profit or loss	11,675
31/12/X9	Bank	10,800			
31/12/X9	Accrued expenses	275			
		11,675			11,675

(c) The amount to be transferred to the statement of profit or loss for administration expenses will be £1,200 greater than the figure in (a).

Admin expenses will show as a debit in the statement of profit or loss in the general ledger.

(d)

Account	£	Dr	Cr
Revenue	9,690		9,690
Discounts allowed	150	150	
SLCA	4,380	4,380	
Bank overdraft	350		350
Accruals			275
Prepayments		1,500	
Administration		5,250	
Selling		11,675	

(e)

A   Objectivity and confidentiality

Objectivity as Vernon has a conflict of interest – which client is he representing? Confidentiality as it would be very hard for Vernon not use the knowledge he has for one company when arguing for the other's position.

TASK 1.4

(a)

Journal	Dr	Cr
Irrecoverable debts	675	
SLCA		675

(b)

Journal	Dr	Cr
Loan account	1,500	
Suspense		1,500

(c)

Journal	Dr	Cr
Closing inventory SFP	26,250	
Closing inventory SPL		26,250

(d)

Journal	Dr	Cr
VAT	360	
Suspense		360
VAT	360	
Suspense		360

(e)

	Ledger balances		Adjustments	
	Dr	Cr	Dr	Cr
Allowance for doubtful debts		625		
Bank	5,500			
Closing inventory (SFP)			26,250	
Closing inventory (SPL)				26,250
Depreciation	3,750			
Irrecoverable debts			675	
Loan		10,000	1,500	
Loan Interest	500			
Accumulated depn plant and machinery		22,750		
Revenue		255,500		
Sales ledger control	29,550			675
Suspense	2,220			1,500 + 720
VAT account		5,400	720	

TASK 1.5

(a)

Adjustment	Amount £	Debit	Credit
		(✓ as appropriate)	
(i) Adjustment 1	150		✓
(ii) Adjustment 2	27		✓
(iii) Adjustment 4	3,550	✓	

(b)

Subsidiary purchases ledger accounts are kept to: (tick the appropriate answer) (1 mark)

Summarise the total purchases	
Show how much suppliers owe in total	
Show much is owed to individual suppliers	✓
Enable the preparation of customer statements	

A Purchases Ledger Control account will show at any time in an accounting period: (tick appropriate answer) (1 mark)

How much each individual payable owes	
How much is owed in total to credit suppliers	✓
How much the total purchases have been in the period	
How many customers' accounts are overdue	

(c)

	Ledger balances		Adjustments		Statement of profit or loss		Statement of financial position	
	Dr	Cr	Dr	Cr	Dr	Cr	Dr	Cr
Capital		50,000						50,000
Bank Loan		10,000						10,000
Non-current assets (Cost)	85,400						85,400	
Opening inventory	2,250				2,250			
Closing inventory			2,100	2,100		2,100	2,100	
Bank	3,125						3,125	
Cash	375						375	
Irrecoverable debts	600				600			
Allowance for doubtful debts		875						875
Depreciation	15,875				15,875			
Sales ledger control	5,500						5,500	
Purchase ledger control		3,750						3,750
Revenue		118,750				118,750		
Purchases	45,625				45,625			
Motor expenses	4,875		125		5,000			
Insurance	1,875			375	1,500			
Office expenses	1,125		250		1,375			
Wages	17,500		125		17,625			
Drawings	30,750						30,750	
Accumulated depreciation		31,750						31,750
Accruals				250				250
Pre-payments			375				375	
Suspense	250			250				
Profit/Loss					31,000			31,000
	£215,125	£215,125	£2,975	£2,975	120,850	120,850	127,625	127,625